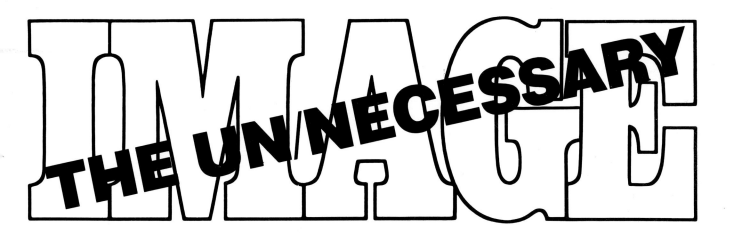

IMAGE
THE UNNECESSARY

EDITED BY
PETER D'AGOSTINO
ANTONIO MUNTADAS

for the
MIT Committee on the
Visual Arts

TANAM PRESS NEW YORK 1982

ISBN 0-934378-30-4

Library of Congress Catalog Card No. 82-51275

Tanam Press
40 White Street
New York, NY 10013

This project involves artists as critics and curators, commentators and creators. Antonio Muntadas and Peter D'Agostino were invited to propose a topic around which a Hayden Corridor Gallery exhibition could be organized. The intention of the invitation was to make curatorial use of the two artists' long term engagement with various communication models and systems. Their understanding of the potency of emerging technologies was particularly informed and acute since both artists have used these technologies as a medium as well as an area worthy of study. We agreed the exhibition would focus on the interrelationship of art, advertising and technology; the congruence of these areas provided a rich arena for artistic scrutiny.

As the artists began to speak with others involved with similar issues—collaborators from a number of countries and backgrounds—the project evolved in scope and format. Essentially, the exhibition became a major publication, the funds for which were supplied by the National Endowment for the Arts through its Visual Artists Forum program. This publication is not a documentation of objects included in a temporary exhibition; rather, each artist was asked to contribute a piece which responded to the publication's theme and format.

Kathy Halbreich
Director of Exhibitions

Contents

Preface

The Un/Necessary Image is a volume of works by artists who are concerned with the "public image" generated by mass media, advertising and communication systems.

The title alludes to an existing dichotomy between public and personal significance, insofar as the meaning of the public image ultimately depends on the context in which it is presented. Determinations of what is "necessary" and "unnecessary" are based on cultural, socio-political, and economic factors, as well as individual value and use.

Historically, the reciprocal influences of modern art movements on styles of advertising, and mass culture's effect on contemporary art forms is well documented. Rather than reiterating these formal similarities, the emphasis of this book is art which deals with the content and meaning of public information.

Utilizing methods ranging from critical analysis and commentary to forms of direct appropriation and deconstruction, the artists offer readings and re-readings of commonly recognizable information in the public domain. As a consequence, these works provide new ways of looking at ourselves within the context of mass culture.

Peter D'Agostino
Antonio Muntadas

UNIVERSAL

MONA LISA
Paris, Louvre

MAN

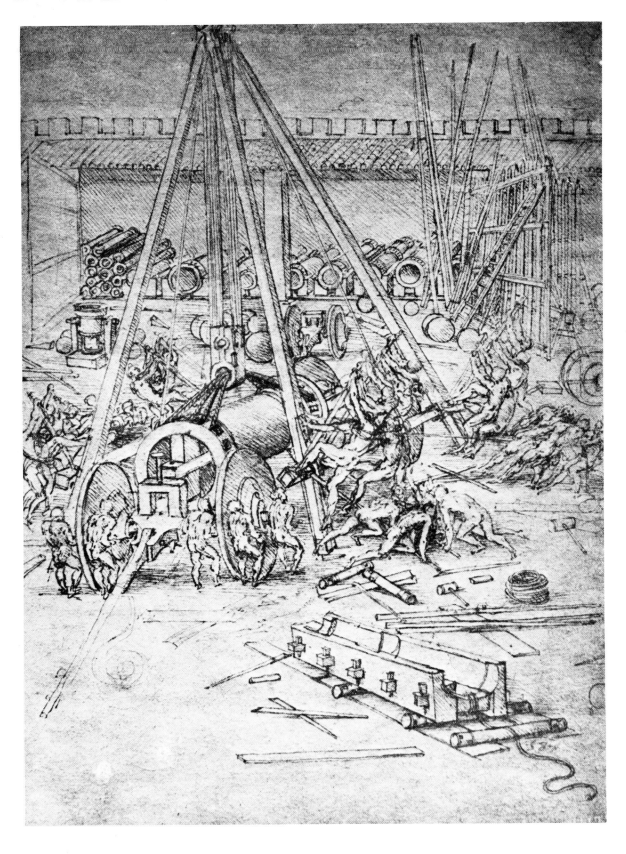

ARSENAL
Windsor Castle

Da Pomellato, i nuovi colori preziosi. Per il polso, la catena con brillanti e rubini. Per il collo, brillanti e i granati - di taglio esclusivo - legati in oro, e il sautoir in perle e lapislazzuli, o giade o corallo. Boccole ovali in oro lucido. Decisamente invitanti.

Decisamente.

POMELLATO
Amica

SOCIETY

MICON
NATO

BIG PAL

It was announced today in a special press conference at the Kennedy Space Center in Florida that NASA and McDonald's Corporation, the fastfood hamburger chain, have entered into a partnership to initiate a new space program for the 1980's. Initial response to the agreement has been enthusiastic, and business leaders as well as politicians are hailing this unprecedented collaboration between a private corporation and a government agency as the wave of the future.

The program, which has been affectionately nicknamed "Big Pal" by the news media, calls for the giant telescope at Mt. Palomar Observatory in California to be dismantled and then re-assembled in outer space on board a space station orbiting the earth. Once the re-assembly is completed, technicians will return to earth and rockets will be fired to propel the space station out of the earth's orbit. It will fly by the outer planets of our solar system and then on into deep space, never to return. The spacecraft will carry new electronic equipment which will allow high quality color photographs taken through the telescope to be transmitted back to earth at the rate of one every twenty-four seconds for the next forty years. Under the terms of the agreement, NASA will use the images for scientific research while McDonald's will own all commercial rights to the images.

McDonald's plan is to broadcast the images live in all of its fastfood family restaurants which will be extensively remodeled with space-age decor, including tilt-back chairs, seat belts, and giant video screens. A McDonald's spokesman said, "When you walk into a new McDonald's, it will be dark and cool and there will be the ambience of high technology. You will be able to purchase your meal and sit down for a ride in outer space. We want people to associate the idea of buying a Big Mac hamburger with space exploration."

Both parties expressed satisfaction with the terms of the agreement. McDonald's feels that their new spaceship restaurants with live images from outer space will give them the competitive edge in the tough fastfood hamburger marketplace; NASA claims that the partnership will give their public image a boost and allow them to take on a new project which they otherwise would not have been able to afford.

What Do You Know When You Know a Picture?

The rhetoric of self-congratulation notwithstanding, art, and of course *art making*, is a pre-eminently behavioral phenomenon animated by pervasively traditional conventions of signification. Lacking a controlling essence, art may be said to "mirror" society precisely because it is responsive to its embodying cultural complex and utterly dependent.

It is for this reason that the imageries of the mass media, of popular and commercial culture, are to be understood to be distinct from the imagery of high art only in degree; for the intentions of neither are meant to be misunderstood; both intend to signify, perhaps even to mean something, and both bend to the bias and limitation of a relatively homogeneous audience.

Hence the tenacity of representational imagery and, coincidentally, the locus of its perverse genius; for in order to be readable at all, even at the menial level of mere identification, images must operate—in every instance—with reference to historically specific conventions of representation and portrayal; and such conventions are inescapably ideological. So in every visual image which may be said to be iconographic there exists a residual, but nonetheless fundamental, didacticism. For images define words; shade, color, texture, and delineate the otherwise elusive identity of that morpho-phonemic thing.

Once having seen the Disney images of *The Three Little Pigs*, that famous title can never again be read as a semantically neutral designation; nor can it again operate *merely* as an indicative clause, such as, for instance, "those four small tape worms." Established now within the iconographic tradition of the pop-modern fabliaux, the Disney Piggies have become a vernacular reference. Like the Mona Lisa, the Lone Ranger, or Grant Wood's sadly shop-worn couple, they are cultural properties, quasi-linguistic real estate, whose ostensibly unique characteristics are there to be milked and manipulated by association.

It is in this respect that the mass media mediates.

The process is a common one and part of the assimilative system by which the charismatic novelties of identity, the idiosyncratically unique make-up of ostensibly discrete—or simply "new" —images are translated into the conventions of public voice. A little like slang, metaphorical surely, and of course akin to poetry, an image that in some sense represents a specific identity —Michelangelo's *David*, for example, or Bugs Bunny—such an image continues to live, to be emblematically alive, precisely to the degree that its application can be made to transcend the boundaries of its original sphere of denotation.

In the jargon of semiotics this refers to an image whose fundamental operation as a sign has been radically rerouted in order to refocus the thrust of its operation as a signifier. At its simplest when we say "turkey" to mean "incompetent"—or, for that matter, when we say "beautiful" to indicate that things have worked out exceptionally well, this process, as remarked by the Metaphysical Poets of the 17th Century, amounts to little more, essentially, than bringing apparently unrelated elements into a *believable* conjunction.

A common technique for the making of metaphor, in the visual arts this is probably most evident in the art of the political cartoon, in satire generally, and of course in those forms of caricature requiring that a maximum of clearly implied information be established through an absolute minimum of means: So Henry Kissinger, swaddled into his very own seamless Superman's suit, rockets skyward from the cover of *Newsweek*, and who, indeed, will miss the meaning of the metaphor?

Yet to describe this process as "metaphorical" is to say virtually nothing, for that designation is both hopelessly broad and excessively simple; and its unqualified usage obscures the crucial fact that words and pictures *work* differently, are not equivalent, operate in fundamentally different kinds of contextual structures, and do not—*and can not*—signify with the same kind of specificity. For in the "normal" process of daily use any word, simply by virtue of its context, may be taken so far from its lexical root that its referential relationship to the "meaning" of the root becomes functionally irrelevant. It is simply not important that the Anglo-Saxon noun, *stane*, lies in the shadowy background of *stone* when that word is used in such idiomatic phrases as "I got stoned" or "He was stone broke," for, excepting the probable existence of a vaguely connotative connection, the word as it is used here has been utterly separated from its historical referent. If I speak of my wife as a "tough fox" neither the adjective, *tough*, nor the noun, *fox*, needs to be defined in terms of etymological source; but, on the other hand, we could not hope to make sense of such visually idiomatic constructions as the *Big Bad Wolf*, *Snoopy*, or *Donald Duck*, if it were not clear that they were conventional visual locutions whose individual configurations refer back to very specific animals while also relying on the generalization of human forms.

Varying with the degree to which it is designed to be explicitly identifiable, all visual imagery is thus inextricably tied to an informing, limiting, or conditioning referent. In the Comics, most film, in much present day salon photog-

BVD.
THE GREAT AMERICAN FIT
FOR THE GREAT AMERICAN MALE.

the individual figures; their sociological status, literary significance, and allegorical function; the iconography of the landscape, its historical "meaning" and, of course, the Protestant interpretation of the Catholic dogma concerning the Latin tradition of the mythological Icarus; each and all are representative of the kinds of information with which we must be intimately conversant before we can even begin to properly see Breughel's painting. Or, for that matter, any other image system whose components derive their meaning from a source beyond the functional frame of reference of the viewer.

Often, however, the "point" of an image is unclear, obscure, or ambiguous simply because the artist fails to provide the kind of specifically indicative syntactic structure that one must have in order to determine precisely what is or is not relevant in the history or background of the items within the iconographic complex. In Robert Frank's book, *The Americans*, is it important that the central figure in the photograph captioned "Convention Hall—Chicago" (#51) is Adlai Stevenson, or that the image on the poster worn by the speaker in "Political Rally—Chicago" (#3) is Estes Kefauver? Not much. But it is important to know *that*. It is important to be able to assign weight and value and relative significance to the individual items within the frame. To know, in short, when imagery has, in fact, become iconography.

Although our understanding of visual imagery is always dependent on our ability to come to terms with the conventions informing its pictorial structure, it is also important to remember that even the most convention-bound image will also almost always be much more than a mere representation, an encoded copy; for unlike words, a visual image—at least in the sense that I have been using that term—always exists as a thing-in-itself. A potentially signifying words such as *tree* may also function as a neutral reference to a category, or class, of objects; or, as Plato would probably have had us believe, it may be the verbal sign for the very *idea* of "treeness." But the visual image is always—always—a concretely physical entity. And its characteristics, *whatever they may be*, will always endow the image with an irreduceable integrity, an identity whose texture and presence will in turn become the essential nexus of its existential condition—of, in short, its being.

In this sense every cohesive image is also a conditioning participant in its own context; and while any image may certainly be radically recontextualized, none is ever so malleable, never so neutral, as the most adamantine word. Simply because words don't have any style, and pictures do.

So it is at this point that we must confront the brute intrusion of style; for it is style—the irrationally self-indulgent, anti-intellectual, and

raphy, and in all figurative painting, there is always something—and often a lot—implicitly referential in the *structure* of the image. And it is this, and not simply the stylistics of the image, that we must explicate if we are to understand the image as an ideological phenomenon. This is all the more important because so much of the imagery of both contemporary popular culture and the commercial media derives its power from the subtle, radical, or simply systemic recontextualization of familiar artifacts. For obvious examples one thinks of the advertising campaign for BVD—*The Great American Fit For The Great American Male*—for Marlboro or Camel cigarettes and their obvious but enormously successful mystification of the paraphernalia popularly associated with the fictional west, the frontier, or, in the case of Winstons, the gay/macho fantasy of hard-hat field and construction work.

For the uninitiated reader this is of course insidiously troublesome, but it is a problem hardly limited to the pictorial arena of overt persuasion; for insofar as any representation is tied to the history of the object it represents, there arises an immediate question as to how much of the object's history is required for an understanding of the significance of the pictorial system. As I've remarked elsewhere, we can't do much more than make a pallid and random sense from such "familiar" paintings as Breughel's *Landscape With The Fall of Icarus* unless we happen to have access to at least a modestly specialized body of knowledge: the identity of

13   Joan Brumfield

utterly untranslatable element of style—that provides the magic glue, that creates the visual cohesion of the image system in a pictorial structure.

In language—in prose fiction, poetry, and the essay—it is the function of grammar to provide verbal images with a cohesive contextual structure and, in the process, guarantee some degree of sense. But in the visual arts style frequently does much more; for insofar as it is pervasive and continuous, style easily becomes the dominant visual element, often overwhelming the identity of the objects it ostensibly represents and, moreover, conditioning and transforming the thrust of their meaning. It is, in this regard, the style of Rouault or Beardsley that is at the heart of the matter. And, indeed, it is style above all else that allows us room and ground to attempt to discuss the implications of the distinctions between, say, the *trees* of Atget, Cezanne, Ansel Adams, and George Herriman. For styles too have their "vocabularies" and their idioms; thus their readability, their apparent meaning. The obviously pointed differences in iconography notwithstanding, it is the significance of the style of Donatello's *David* that sets it so distinctly apart from the *David* of Rubens or Verrocchio.

Of course, to the degree that it establishes or operates within a convention, style itself may be said to be iconographic. But not irrevocably fixed, for insofar as it is in conformity with a convention whose attributes reinforce, or may be rationalized into, the value system of the dominant class, the longevity of the image will often involve a continuous process of recontextualization. So we discover Michelangelo's *David* to be solidly within the mainstream of the Heroic Tradition and Verrochio's, by contrast, to be tangentially eccentric; and indeed, Michelangelo's image is *everywhere*. Appropriated by post-card photographers, dime-store decorators, advertising illustrators, and plaster-casters, the image seems virtually omnipresent. Whereas we see Donatello's only occasionally. We look at Verrochio's for comparison, at Rembrandt's only as specialists, and at Rubens' *David* never.

Yet the point is that while style renders meaning and the sociology of convention informs it, the medium of art is art itself; the reservoir of the accessible past, which one may draw upon as one draws upon the stuff of language. Unconfined by grammar, rich with tradition, enormously variable, and geographically transcendent as no national language has ever been the potential persuasive power of visual imagery seems inexhaustible.

But there is yet another point to be made, for the agency of that power is rhetorical only. Lacking the elements of a grammar, the syntactic structure of an exclusively visual system can never transcend the limitations of its fundamentally gestural nature. For example: In Walker Evans' 1935 photograph captioned "West Virginia Miner's House," it would seem preposterous to suppose that the over-size window displays decorating that impoverished interior are not meant to be read as tendentiously recontextualized symbols within an economically pathetic environment. Consider the evidence. It is, after all, pretty much the bottom of the Depression. Nearly one person in five is unemployed and no hope in sight. Conditions in rural areas are desperate, especially in the South where in some communities unemployment approaches nearly ninety per-cent, and while the worst years may now be past, the obvious want of this poor patched interior speaks to a condition in contrast to which the images of these confident graduates and that cheery Santa are hardly mute.

As always Evans' composition is scrupulous and precise. The scene is organized before us in modulated rectilinear planes, the dominant wall parallel to the picture plane and centered between the ⅓ – ⅔ division of the ceiling above and the floor below. Like much of the lower wall the latter is rough, worn, and dirty, a bare plank floor partially covered by a tattered piece of carpet. The ceiling and the rest of the wall is constructed of ancient wall board and a sagging patchwork of disassembled cardboard boxes. On our left, but barely discernible, is an apparently haphazard clutter of furniture. A broom, dirty and upended, leans against the wall and, carefully centered in what becomes the dominant figure group of the composition, a crudely beautiful bentwood rocker sits below two stand-up advertisements taken from what was once a drugstore window display. The images are remarkable. On the left, ceremoniously in traditional cap and gown, two new graduates stride from the top of the world into the future. Beneath their neatly polished shoes is a map of the United States. They are stereotypically clean featured and smiling. And they are models of decorum. Appropriately, the woman rests her left hand on the cradled arm of her male companion while displaying her rolled diploma with the other. The man, of course, gestures to The World with his. He is answered, compositionally, by one of the most stereotypically paternal of all Santas who, facing the viewer, raises a bottle of Coca-Cola in a parallel salute, matching, in the best of Renaissance symmetries, the triangulating pattern of the opposing figure.

So the socio-political connotations of the iconography seems to be obvious and the "layered ironies" unavoidable; yet a question persists: For all the possible implications suggested by the imagery, what can we legitimately claim to know that we know once we think we know this image? What can we verifiably assert that the

Walker Evans *West Virginia Miner's House* 1935

picture means or, for that matter, says? For the significance of the apparent distinction between one man's tree, or shepherd, or villain and another's can never be explicitly verifiable except as probabilities derived from inferential extrapolations from convention, from the specificity of allusion, and from the historical implications of connotative association. And while the gesture of style, the juxtaposition of elements, the organization of parts in a painting or a photograph may appear to approach the structural possibilities of a simple declarative sentence, they can never truly approximate it.

The imagery associated with the atrocities of war, the death of Marat, the rape of the Sabine women, the bombing of Hiroshima and Nagasaki may operate, perhaps, as pseudo-statements suggesting that this situation is bad, good, a rip-off or a turn-on or an outrage, but such imagery can only be effectively persuasive if the viewer is uncritically susceptible to the rhetoric of the system or prepared to be convinced.

Of course, an iconography of implication can be ideologically pointed simply by virtue of framing and the compositional syntax of its visual system; but that's part of the point; that's part of the problem. For as ostensibly eloquent an artist as Walker Evans may be, his actual syntax remains merely compositional, not grammatical: such is the nature of the medium. And for that reason, exclusively visual imagery is, and must be, absolutely incapable of developing an expository elucidation of even the most rudimentary sort.

And that is why, unable to speak with authority in the world, the visual arts will continue to remain the indifferent plaything of curators and collectors and the most favored instrument of the most socially sophisticated of liars and thieves.

Revised from an essay originally published in the *LAICA Journal* © 1982 John Brunfield

On Social Grease

1975
Excerpts. Entire work consists of 6 plaques, each 30 x 30",
photoengraved magnesium plates, mounted on aluminum.
First exhibited at John Weber Gallery, New York, 1975.

Photos: John Russel

Perhaps the most important single reason for the increased interest of international corporations in the arts is the almost limitless diversity of projects which are possible.

These projects can be tailored to a company's specific business goals and can return dividends far out of proportion to the actual investment required.

C. Douglas Dillon

C. Douglas Dillon
Metropolitan Museum, Chairman
Business Committee for the Arts, Co-founder, first Chairman
Rockefeller Foundation, Chairman (1972-75)
Brookings Institution, Chairman (1970-76)
United States and Foreign Securities Corporation, Director, Chairman
Secretary of the Treasury (1961-65)
Dillon, Read and Company, Chairman of Executive Committee, Director

Quoted from C. Douglas Dillon
"Cross-Cultural Communication Through the Arts," in *Columbia Journal of World Business*,
Columbia University, New York, September/October 1971

17 Hans Haacke

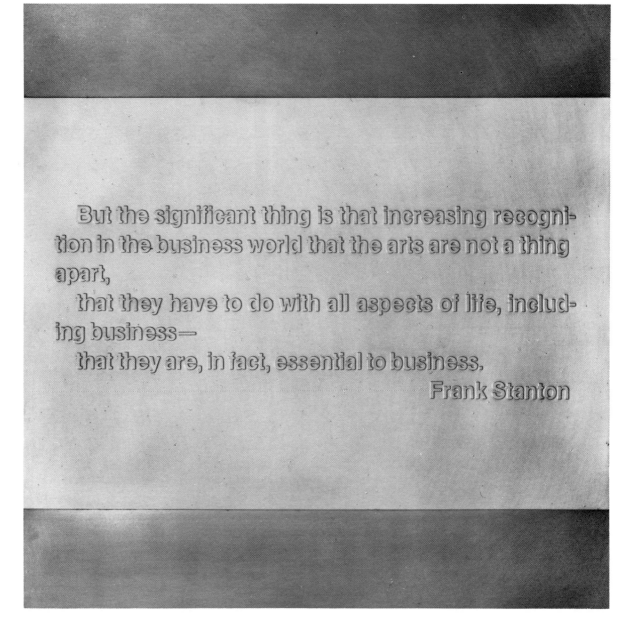

Frank Stanton
Business Committee for the Arts, Chairman (1971-73)
Carnegie Institution, Washington, D.C., Chairman
Atlantic Richfield Company, Director
American Electric Power Company, Inc., Director
CBS, Inc., President (1946-71)
Interpublic Group, Director
New Perspective Fund, Director
New York Life Insurance Company, Director
Pan American World Airways, Inc., Director
Simplicity Pattern Company, Director

Quoted from Frank Stanton
"The Arts – A Challenge to Business," speech to 25th Anniversary Public Relations Conference
of Public Relations Society of American and Canadian Public Relations Society
Detroit, November 12, 1972

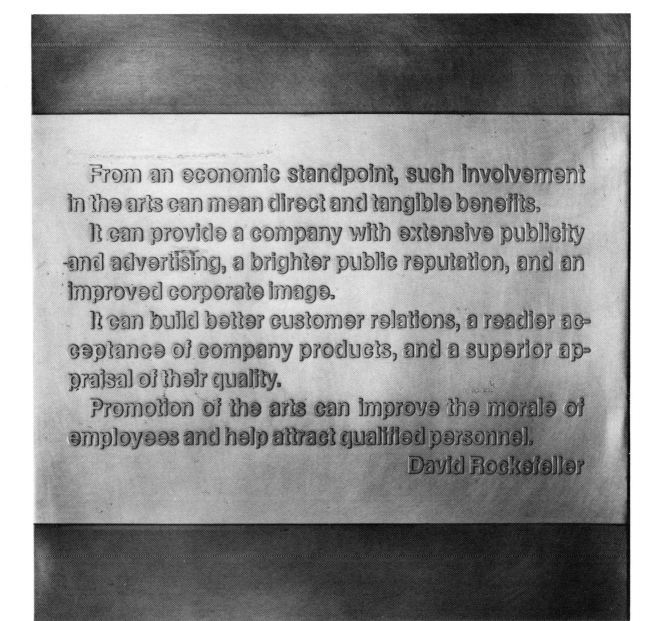

From an economic standpoint, such involvement in the arts can mean direct and tangible benefits.

It can provide a company with extensive publicity and advertising, a brighter public reputation, and an improved corporate image.

It can build better customer relations, a readier acceptance of company products, and a superior appraisal of their quality.

Promotion of the arts can improve the morale of employees and help attract qualified personnel.

David Rockefeller

David Rockefeller
Museum of Modern Art, Vice Chairman
Business Committee for the Arts, Co-founder and Director
Chase Manhattan Bank Corporation, Chairman (1969-1981)
Council on Foreign Relations, Chairman

Quoted from David Rockefeller
"Culture and the Corporation's Support of the Arts," speech to National Industrial Conference Board
September 20, 1966

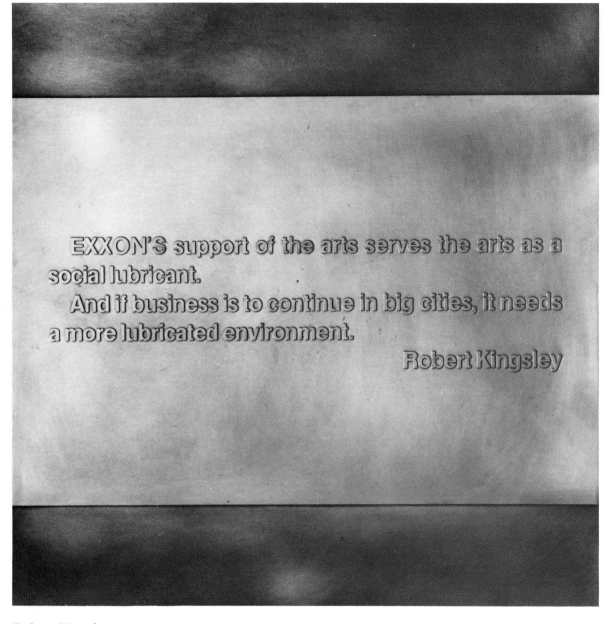

EXXON'S support of the arts serves the arts as a
social lubricant.
    And if business is to continue in big cities, it needs
a more lubricated environment.

                                     Robert Kingsley

Robert Kingsley
Exxon Corporation, New York, Manager of Urban Affairs in Department of Public Affairs
Arts and Business Council, New York, President
Died 1980

Quoted in Marylin Bender
"Business Aids the Arts . . . And Itself," *The New York Times*, October 20, 1974, section III, page 1

Hans Haacke's 'Cunning Involvement'

The Dadaists attached much less importance
to the sales value of their work than to its
uselessness for contemplative immersion. . . .
What they intended and achieved was a re-
lentless destruction of the aura of their
creations. . . .

— Walter Benjamin

In works such as *On Social Grease* (1975),
Hans Haacke uses an aspect of art which the
Dada movement tried to destroy. Instead of
making anti-art in an effort to force
consideration of the social alienation which
caused it, Haacke has sought to make art
useless as a cultural alibi by attacking the
context — what Walter Benjamin termed the
"aura"[1] — which sanctifies art. Unlike the
flamboyantly aggressive anti-art of Tristan
Tzara, et al., Haacke creates a cool non-art so
seemingly insubstantial that the aura of it becomes the center of focus — and, more impor-
tantly, of controversy. As such, Haacke
deftly uses what the nihilistic Dadaists
merely tried to negate. The result is a negative dialectic whereby Haacke affirms the
process of artistic enshrinement, though only
in order to debunk it. In *On Social Grease*,
Haacke uses remarks about art he did not
utter, without any overt comments of his
own, in an aesthetic realm he has not made.
Thus, the art world has been faced with the
irony of appropriating its modes of art appropriation, even while proclaiming art's
purity — its distance from all else.

To consider Haacke's *On Social Grease*
simply mounted journalism is to be unduly
naive about an art exhibit's lack of neutrality.
What makes Haacke's choice of quotations
art is the quasi-religious context — what he
calls the "devotional atmosphere" — in which
his irreverent work is placed. In turn,
Haacke's selection of quotations attests to the
existence of this atmosphere by advocating
the exploitation of it. This is why Haacke has
maintained that his work can be understood
fully only when it is experienced in a museum-
like setting. In contradistinction to Berkeley's
esse=percipi world, this aesthetic realm depends for its absolute existence not on an
a-historical deity, but on the all too historical
demands of corporate capitalism. Marcel
Duchamp's *readymades* disclosed the provi-

sional nature of art — to a large extent a.
its own context; Hans Haacke's work has
posed the provisional quality of art's contex
— it is as extensively recognized as society
allows it to be.

The quotations of *On Social Grease* are presented with an adroit impersonality that is
underscored by the metallic precision of these
photo-engraved magnesium plates mounted
on aluminum. Because the six plaques look
like memorial plates they can perhaps be seen
as subtle allusions to the mortality of these
purportedly timeless statements. The formal
reticence of Haacke's work recalls Gilbert
Lascault's contention that the "cool look constitutes a criticism of art itself . . . it has
voluntarily discarded its prestige."[2]
Furthermore, the quotations themselves show
that corporations are far less respectful of art
than their esteem would seem to indicate.
Implicit in the cult of art which originated
with *l'art pour l'art* was a reaction against the
vulgar practicality of bourgeois society, as de-
nounced by Baudelaire in his "Salon of 1846,"
— a view which derived from Kant's notion of
art as involving "Zweckmässigkeit ohne
Zweck" (Purposiveness without purpose).[3]
Explicit in *On Social Grease* is another
position altogether. In this six part work (4 of
which are shown here). C. Douglas Dillon,
David Rockefeller, Frank Stanton, and Robert
Kingsley all emphasize that art is a means to
good business — "a social lubricant" — rather
than an end in itself. Yet at the same time
this art is useful because of its presumed uselessness. Art's exalted state, partly a result of
its supposed distance from the utilitarian, is
used to sanctify the corporations which
promote it. Oscar Wilde's contention that "All
art is quite useless" is quietly ignored by
patrons like David Rockefeller, who is quoted
in plaque four of *On Social Grease*: "It [Art]
can provide a company with extensive publicity and advertising, a brighter public reputation, and an improved corporate image."

As Haacke further shows in a more recent work, *Upstairs at Mobil* (1981), a brighter public image has been purchased by Mobil Oil and other corporations. The use of art patronage as self-advertisement has been an effective component of Mobil's efforts to legitimate its unethical practices. One of Haacke's pieces in his Mobil series is *Creating Consent*, which consists of a metallic oil drum crested by a TV antenna, with the caption: "We spent $102 million last year in advertising. . . . We just want to be heard." Thus, Haacke calls attention to the paradoxical position of Mobil: on the one hand, Mobil pretends merely to believe in a public dialogue; yet on the other hand, it exploits the private ownership of the so-called public media to engage in a monologue. This self-serving and anti-democratic monologue is designed to monopolize "mass" communication, as well as to manufacture a misinformed public consensus about its real aims. Mobil's patronage of art exhibitions is a major way of "creating consent" by using art to convey something other than what the art was conceived to express.

Nowhere has this policy of using art been more unabashedly endorsed that in the May 1979 issue of *Art News*, which has a special section on "The Corporate Patrons." The seven articles in this section show that Corporations have gone from spending 22 million dollars on art in 1965 to more than 250 million dollars in 1978. Contributions by Exxon and four other companies have been so extensive that PBS has been dubbed the Petroleum Broadcasting Company, and a museum salute to this spending has resulted in a large exhibition: "Art Inc.: American Painting from Corporate Collections," which includes paintings owned by thirty different American corporations. One major patron even states that "Bringing the arts to the people is the core of the capitalist system."[4] As if to consummate this lucrative, yet ill-sorted relationship, *Art News* informs us in another section of this same issue (p. 162) that in the last five years it has become the fastest-growing art magazine, while at the same increasing its advertising more than any other art publication. Thus, the cycle appears closed: selling art equals marketing legitimacy; buying art translates into purchasing social reprieves.

One of Mobils major assets is Herb Schmertz, our public relations genius and house philosopher.

It was Herb who made Mobil a columnist of The New York Times. It was Herb who turned PBS into what our enemies call the Petroleum Broadcasting Service. And it was Herb who masterminded our entry into the art world. All this and more for little over $21 million annually.

Herb's Democratic Party background and his connection to the Kennedys ... He speaks their language and knows how to keep [the] balance when ... their support. This will be easier under the Reagan administration ... [We] just bought the Croton-Cortland News, as another outlet for the Mobil word. The two also tried themselves as novelists.

Takeover is a racy book about big business, corruption, and sex. They [dedicated it to] an endangered species, the "free-market system."

Mobil makes my money grow!

Mobils public relations people make a killing through the support of the arts.

Although our tax-deductible contributions are hardly equal to 0.1 percent of our profits, they have bought us extensive good will in the world of culture.

More important, however, opinion leaders and politicians now listen to us when we speak out on taxes, government regulations, and crippling environmentalism.

The secret of getting so much mileage out of a minimal investment is twofold: a developed sense for high-visibility projects at low cost and well-funded campaigns to promote them. Mobil, in fact, ranks lowest among the 50 companies which give most in proportion to their pretax profits.

Museums now hesitate to exhibit works which conflict with our views, and we need not cancel grants as we did at Columbia's Journalism School. The art world has earned our support: "Art is energy in its most beautiful form!"

Mobil makes my money grow!

Excerpts from
Upstairs at Mobil: Musings of a Shareholder

The ideological position involved in the wedding of art and corporate spending is most effective, however, when it is least apparent. Significantly, Haacke has generated considerable controversy by making this contradiction the subject of his art. In the spring of 1971 Haacke's art was openly censored by the Guggenheim Museum, because one of his works scheduled for exhibit there, *Shapolsky et al Manhattan Real Estate Holdings, a Real Time Social System, as of May 1, 1971*, disclosed unsavory business activities in slum ownership. The *cause celèbre* which resulted from cancellation of his show made Haacke's piece more effective—or rather extended the scope of its anti-aura—by making the public more aware of the museum's self-serving concern with art. Furthermore, one of Haacke's most important works deals explictly with the corporate affiliations of the Guggenheim's Board of Trustees. First exhibited at the Stefanotti Gallery in March 1974, the seven glass-covered, brass-framed panels of *Solomon R. Guggenheim Museum Board of Trustees* feature the same formal taciturnity as Haacke's other works. The information transmitted makes clear why American corporations are trying to cleanse themselves through purist art. Panel five shows, for example, that three of the Guggenheim trustees are on the Board of Directors of the Kennecott Copper Corporation, whose sympathy for the neo-fascist Pinochet is well-known.[5]

Another work by Haacke, *Manet-PROJEKT'74*, engendered a nation-wide controversy in Germany when it was banned from the Wallraf-Richartz-Museum in Cologne, after having been commended at first by the curator of modern art. This work deals with the social status of those who owned Manet's *Bunch of Asparagus* (1880) before it entered the Wallraf-Richartz and with the pecuniary rewards this ownership reaped for each person. In rejecting Haacke's *Manet-PROJEKT'74*, the director of the museum said, "A museum knows nothing about economic power; it does indeed, however, know something about spiritual power."[6] Similarly, a reaction by Robert Kingsley, one of the six men quoted in *On Social Grease* (1975), reveals at least a rudimentary awareness that the contradictions of corporate patronage cannot withstand Haacke's scrutiny. When *On Social Grease* was on display at the John Weber Gallery in May 1975, Kingsley's secretary saw the show and expressed concern about the exhibit. Nonetheless, Kingsley came to the Weber Gallery the next day—apparently confident that the work really wasn't *that* harmful—and had his photograph taken with his statement.

Creating Consent
1981
Oildrums, TV antenna
73 x 23 x 23"
Photo: Jon Abbott

Corporate patronage makes the artist an indentured master—a servant of the corporate system, he is master only of his art. Ironically, it is in conceding to this conformity, that many artists feel most free. Able to create "independently," these artists ignore the dependence into which corporate money helps force them. Because art is located at the summit of the culture complex, however, it appears detached from the ordinary world anyway. By purchasing and controlling art, business leaders seek to accrue by association some of the loftiness attributed to art. In this sense art is used to support artificial social hierarchies. Furthermore, by buying art—if not the artist's silence—corporate magnates are better able to monopolize interpretations of art even while they support the myth that art is above interpretation. The second plate of *On Social Grease* aptly makes this point by quoting Nelson Rockefeller: "I am not really concerned with what the artist means, it is not an intellectual operation—it is what I feel."

By warning that "artists are not better than other people," Haacke has emphasized the complicity, inadvertent or otherwise, of many artists in this process of commercialization.[7] Since the most important thing for many artists is fame, rather than understanding (although Borges was doubtlessly right to call fame a form of incomprehension), these artists accept, even expect, the lack of understanding their "transcendental" art induces. Even while they are afflicted by a glamorous pathos of distance, many artists endorse the mystique of art which in turn makes it more susceptible to corporate intimacy. Fortunately, Haacke's recalcitrant art shows that while artists must work *within* corporate society, they need not work *with* this society. Purist artists, unlike Haacke, are paradoxical because they proclaim their art to be what is impossible, i.e., "apolitical." Their paradox is culpable because it is self-induced. Haacke's political commitment remains true, however, even when society disallows the change he seeks to inspire. As Haacke maintains:

"Given the dialectic nature of the contemporary petit-bourgeois consciousness industry, its vast resources probably can be put to use against the dominant ideology. This, however, seems to be possible only with a matching dialectical approach and may very well require a cunning involvement in all the contradictions of the medium and its practitioners."[8]

Haacke's work avoids a failing of the Dadaist belief in pure negativity. Now a chapter in the history of art, the Dada work in a museum context is usually entertaining rather than disruptive—as evidenced by the domesticated 1968 show at the Museum of Modern Art in New York. The extremism of their liberated art has been made to correspond to the Caligulean notions of "freedom" championed by multinational corporations and expected of bohemian artists—most of whom have forgotten that bohemianism originated in part as a life of political parody, a *reductio ad absurdum* of *laissez-faire* society.[9] Like Caligula's, however, this freedom is now at the expense of others, even if it is not without limits. For all their nihilism the Dadas helped unwittingly to entrench an idea of artistic freedom—what Sartre has called artistic irresponsibility[10]—which is now used to proclaim the anarchistic separateness of art, even while tacitly denying it.

Because Haacke has not tried to destroy art but has "dematerialized" it by means of ideas about the way art is viewed, he has been considered a conceptual artist. As Haacke contends, however, this designation is not really accurate. Conceptual artists like Sol Le Witt have stated that once the concept is conceived mentally the art work already exists. Thus, the formal realization of it is predetermined and perfunctory.[11] Conversely, Haacke has dealt in a seemingly perfunctory format with the ideas which make art inevitably different from what artists, even the conceptualists, intended. In a sense, Haacke's work can be termed meta-conceptual art, since he is concerned with the social ideas which not only precede the artist's concept, but influence the way this art will be interpretatively completed.

Edward Kienholz's *The Art Show: Concept Tableau* (1963), which consists of the phrase "The Art Show" photoengraved on a metallic plate, is ostensibly similar to Hans Haacke's *On Social Grease*, with its photoengraved quotations. Unlike Kienholz, however, Haacke does not assert the primacy of the artist's concept, but the dominance of the ambience which awaits this concept. In an effort to combat the reification of art as a commodity and the treatment of art in solely formal terms, conceptual artists like Joseph Kosuth and Douglas Huebler have promoted "objectless" art. Like Haacke's *Guggenheim Trustees*, Kosuth's "information art" consists of statements mounted on panels. While Kosuth has been committed, however, to purging art of market values "by presenting new propositions as to art's nature,"[12] Haacke is interested in radicalizing the market place by advancing propositions about the context which precedes "art's nature."

Connections between Haacke and his countryman Joseph Beuys are even less apparent, in spite of the extensive political controversy Beuys has caused.[13] The leading maker of multiples in modern art, Beuys is also a famous performance artist (which his apocalyptic *Aktions* like "Explaining Pictures to a Dead Hare") and a creator of "de-objectified" art objects like *Fettecke* (corners with globs of animal fat) which are supposed to be too gross to be appropriated easily by the beautiful commercial art world. Nonetheless, Beuys, whose radical mysticism is reminiscent of Artaud's, is too inclined to be a guru of the disaffected. His transreligious concept of *Liebestraum* and his belief that fat is an *Urmasse* show that Beuys (who fasts for some of his *Aktions*) is really a politicized version of Kafka's Hunger Artist — one who scandalizes because of bizarre antics, rather than confronts because of perceptive insights. On the other hand, Haacke has stated that the aim of art should be to foster a critical rather than a devotional attitude concerning the mystique of art which Beuys indirectly supports. Furthermore, Haacke has spoken out against multiples as having "more to do with opening new markets than with democracy."

Significantly, Haacke's works are free of the tendentiousness characteristic of socialist realism. His art does not prescribe unthinking reactions; it inspires critical reflections which lead to thoughtful actions. Unlike propaganda, Haacke's work is not a simple view that loosens reflexes, but the presentation of complex situations that demand choices. As Robert Hobbs has stated, Haacke does not so much interpret art for us, as take it out of dimly lit halls.[15] If Haacke's work offends, this is because society is offensive. For a 1974 show at the Institute of Contemporary Art in London, Haacke was asked to make a statement about the role of a committed artist. He responded by quoting Bertolt Brecht's 1934 remarks about the "Five Difficulties in Writing the Truth.":

". . . the courage to write the truth, although it is being suppressed; the intelligence to recognize it, although it is being covered up; the judgment to choose those in whose hands it becomes effective; the cunning to spread it among them."[16]

First published, in a German translation, in *Kritische Berichte*, Vol. 10, No. 1, 1982.

[1] Walter Benjamin, "The Work of Art in the Age of Mechanical Reproduction" (1936), in *Illuminations*, tran. by H. Zohn, New York, 1969, pp. 221-223. An example of how Dadaist nihilism has been tamed by museums can be found in Harold Rosenberg's "MOMA Dada," *Artworks and Packages*, New York, 1969, pp. 199-212.

[2] Gilbert Lascault, "Contemporary Art and the 'Ole Mole'," in *Art and Confrontation*, tran. by N. Foxell, New York, 1968, p. 70.

[3] John Wilcox, "The Beginnings of l'Art pour l'Art," *Journal of Aesthetics and Art Criticism*, Vol. XI, No. 4, June 1953, pp. 360-377.

[4] Donald Sanders, "Winston-Salem's R. Philip Hanes," *Art News*, Vol. 78, No. 5, May 1979, p. 61.

[5] For a discussion of how the CIA and the U.S. Corporations helped sabotage the Allende government, see the Select Committee to Study Government Operations with Respect to Intelligence Activities of the United States Senate (known as the Church Committee Report), 94th Congress, 1st Session, Vol. 7, *Covert Action*, Dec. 4-5, 1975, p. 170: On September 15, 1970, President Nixon informed CIA director Richard Helms that the democratic election of Allende "would not be acceptable to the United States and instructed the CIA to play a direct role in organizing a military coup d'etat in Chile." Also, see David Kunzle, "Art of the New Chile," in *Art and Architecture in the Service of Politics*, ed. by H. A. Millon and L. Nochlin, MIT Press, 1978, pp. 356-381.

[6] Hans Haacke, *Framing and Being Framed*, N.Y., 1975, p. 72. Also, see Robert Hobbs' review of this book in *Art Journal*, Vol. XXXVI, No. 2, Winter 1977, pp. 176-180.

[7] Hans Haacke, "The Role of Artist in Today's Society," *Art Journal*, Vol. XXXIV, No. 4, Summer 1975, pp. 327-328.

[8] Hans Haacke, "The Constituency," *Tracks*, Vol. 3, No. 3, Fall 1977, p. 105. Also, see David Craven, "A Demographic Look at American Artists," *Artworkers News*, Vol. X, No. 10, June 1981, pp. 22-25.

[9] T. J. Clarke, *Image of the People*, Greenwich, Conn., 1973, p. 34.

[10] Jean-Paul Sartre, *What Is Literature*? (1947), tran. by B. Frechtman, New York, 1965, p. 128-129: ". . . as this systematic destruction never went any further than scandal, this amounted in the last analysis, to saying that the primary duty of the writer was to provoke a *scandal* and that his inalienable right was to escape its consequences."

[11] Sol Le Witt, "Sentences on Conceptual Art," in *Six Years: The Dematerialization of the Art Object from 1966-1972*, ed. by Lucy Lippard, New York, 1973, pp. 75-76. In the "Postface" to this book, Lippard wrote (p. 263): "Hopes that 'conceptual art' would be able to avoid the general commercialization, the destructively 'progressive' approach of modernism were for the most part unfounded . . . There are some exceptions, among them certain works by Haacke."

[12] Joseph Kosuth, "Art After Philosophy I, II" (1969), in *Idea Art*, ed. by G. Battock, New York, 1973, p. 81.

[13] Haacke and Beuys were both in the exhibition *Art into Society: Society into Art, Seven German Artists*, the Institute of Contemporary Arts, London, October 30 – November 24, 1974.

[14] Haacke, "Role of the Artist," p. 328.

[15] Hobbs, *op. cit.*, p. 180.

[16] Catalogue for *Art into Society: Society into Art*, p. 63. See also, Jack Burnham, "Steps in the Formulation of Real-Time Political Art," in *Framing and Being Framed*, New York, p. 140.

COMPUTER

**KNOWS EXACTLY WHERE
EACH BIT OF DATA IS STORED
AND HOW EACH ANSWER
IS OBTAINED**

**REQUIRES OUTSIDE
MAINTENANCE**

VS. BRAIN

HAS NO UNDERSTANDING
OF ITS OWN SYSTEMS OR
METHODS OF OPERATION

SELF-CLEANING

THE LUCIFERIAN MARRIAGE
Government/Corporation/Media "Fact" as Entertainment
A Collage Essay

. . . .There is agreement on the part of the executive authorities not to produce or sanction anything that in any way differs from their own rules, their own ideas about consumers or above all about themselves. . . .The totality of the culture industry has put an end to (expression). . .(It is) exclusively concerned with effects: it crushes insubordination and makes them (expressions) subserve the formula which replaces the work.[1]

Forty years ago when Max Horkheimer and Theodor Adorno analyzed the interdependent structure of corporate bureaucratic aims and their realizations through media systems (film industry, newspaper—the "Culture Industry"), it was not so evident that the "Society of Spectacle"[2] had already been born, nor that its political expression was completely subsumed into the state of mind control and mass deception vividly manifested in life as entertainment.

After the sixties, the illusion shattered and political action and protest unabashedly left the exclusive domain of civics and entered the arena of culture. The assumption that the impact of the media is reversible through subversive symbolic action proved to be a self-deception.

What emerged, however, was a "grammar of interaction"[3] which became the basis for subsequently mythic images of political activism. These images, cliches organically generated by the first generation of newspeople and political radicals to confront the enormous potential for communication immanent in the blossoming electronic technology, remains tied to the bygone era. The actual present is lost for the moment in its own transiency only to be recouped by the static image that has become formula culled from the past. The replacement of the particular for the mythic general becomes the transformative vehicle leading significant political action into insignificant "Entertainment". Diversion serves to pacify and preserve the status quo. That revolutionary potential which survived from the past now can be made to appear as eternally immutable by the present. The picture of a young, blond woman with a head-band handing a daisy to a cop is lifted from the past and reappears on the cover of a 1981 newspaper article. The image, converted into a myth of civil dissent, at best evokes nostalgia but becomes simultaneously the product for derision while it maintains its seat deep in the heart of "the familiar" where it is protected and sustained. Customs are given reception and receive support in the depths of the collective psyche. Now the standards of this formula are so immediately recognizeable because of the levels of public saturation achieved through the past twenty years that the particulars of the present are ground into the generalities of the past making a pasty, blanched dough for future thought.

The state to which political action has degenerated in the public eye and mind is no better represented than in the coverage of the anti-nuclear protest against Pacific Gas & Electric Company's nuclear plant at Diablo Canyon, California. This arena of the cultural was brought vividly to life as the protest was transformed from a unique alternative process of organized, strictly controlled, philosophically grounded action with the largest number of arrests in American anti-nuclear history, into a circus of memories generated by the media, absorbable for the public on the level of public theatre.

Although expression in culture followed by that of political activism has been reduced and subordinated to the domination of government/corporate and media structures, these entities themselves remain intact and continue to control the public imagination. It is no accident that P.G. & E.'s corporate brochure advertising Diablo Canyon Nuclear Information Center refers to the "Nuclear Theatre" and shows a young blond girl—the paragon of vulnerability and innocence perpetuated by a white, Anglo-Saxon dominated technological world—playing with the tools which will lead her into the Nuclear Theatre on its cover. We are persuaded to become spectators of technology, of the mysteries of fission physics where we, embodied in the little girl, remain safely distant from the real plant, its awesome power and destruction between which it and ourselves steps the corporate/government shield. Passive, in a theatre of activity, she/we participate in a world of unseen forces. The language used to convey us there is ostensibly objective, inviting and offers amusement. Lulled into enjoyment, it does not threaten or challenge our behaviour in the way that dissents from the status quo, or attempts to inform us that events or phenomena occurring around us endanger our lives, as much of the anti-nuclear energy/weaponry literature does. The tacit accusation that we are cooperating in our own demise is difficult to fathom when read in the armchair or at the kitchen table of our private lives.

Dr. Helen Caldicott's warning strikes the unreceptive ears of the entertained who have forfeited responsibility as the pariah of doom disturbing their vaccuum:

If you've got a nuclear reactor in your city, your enemy doesn't need a nuclear bomb anymore; all they need to do is drop a conventional weapon on your nuclear reactor. If Europe had been populated with nuclear reactors in the Second World War, it would be still uninhabitable right now. That's the scenario we're setting up.[4]

Since it is the corporate and media union which sets the standards for public information communication, it is very difficult to convey opinions or facts which do not conform to their proscribed systems; systems that have become so embedded in the collective psyche to have become inseparable in a general sense from what individuals believe they understand and need.

During the preparation of and throughout our protest at Diablo Canyon, we intuitively acknowledged that our actions were to become a public mediated commodity, totally controlled and destined for prime-time news and perhaps an article in *Time* or *Newsweek*. The omnipotence of those in power positions controls our dream of participating and actually affecting a system. Robbed of reality's content, our actions are so co-opted that only the impotent idealism remains. Like sleep walkers or actors in film, our content is gone, the illusion lives on as electronic representation. Anyone involved with the media must reconcile themselves to this horrible fact.

The situation of our lobotomized entertainment was never more poetically expressed than by Ivan Chtcheglov in *Formula for a New City*, 1958:

The dark has been driven away by electricity and the seasons by central heating. Night and the summer have lost all their charm and the dawn has gone. Those who live in cities want to withdraw from cosmic reality and all they dream of is ways of doing so. For obvious reasons: dreams begin and end in reality.[5]

Even that reality is the one portrayed by the "producers of experience". The standards of their formula oppress all opposition and wash all particulars into the general producing a murky present and a glassy-eyed "walk-man" future.

While everyone at the Diablo Blockade Encampment was at a consensus meeting, Sandra Koponen had an idea that we two became very excited about: Everyone should quietly pack up and leave the camp in the middle of the night. Just go home without explanation.

In retrospect, I believe in this position even more. There would still be the "Media Corral", the helicopters of television crews and highway patrol flying overhead, the power lines of P.G. & E. hissing and zinging next to the empty camp site, the patrol cars cruising past, the dozens and dozens of waiting buses ready to cart away the protestors, the build up of police forces, the readiness of P.G. & E. (or any other "authority" with power and money to protect their "private property"). Yes, all that capital and investment in power would be poised on the threshhold of anticipation. The whole world would be waiting by the television sets and watching the newsstands for the latest "confrontation," and we would simply slip away. Like the night giving way to the dawn—there would be our negative action of positive renunciation. We would totally refuse to participate in the set-up.

Graffiti is transgressive, not because it substitutes another content, another discourse, but simply because it responds, there, on the spot, and breaches the fundamental role of non-response enunciated by all the media. Does it oppose one code to another? I don't think so: it simply smashes the code. It doesn't lend itself to deciphering as a test rivaling commercial discourse; it presents itself as a transgression. So, for example, the witticism, which is a transgressive reversal of discourse, does not act on the basis of another code as such; it works through the instantaneous deconstruction of the dominant discursive code. It volatilizes the category of the code, and that of the message. This, then, is the key to the problem: by trying to preserve (even as one "dialectically transcends" them) any *separated instances of the structural communication grid*, one obviates the possibility of fundamental change, and condemns oneself to fragile manipulatory practices that would be dangerous to adopt as a "revolutionary strategy." What is strategic in this sense is only what radically checkmates the dominant form.[6]

PG&E
Diablo Canyon
Nuclear Information
Center
San Luis Obispo, California

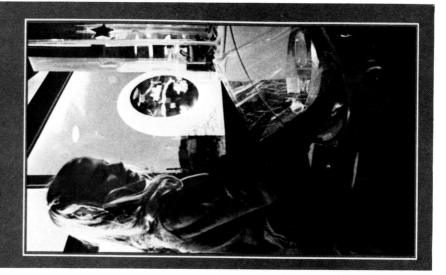

sight, sound and touch combine

in the Diablo Canyon Nuclear Information Center to make an exciting experience that takes you through the past, beneath the sea and into the years to come.

You will be caught in the web of life that connects all living things on land and in the sea with the past and the future.

Take a close-up look at the plants, animals and fish that live in Diablo Canyon and Diablo Cove. Enjoy the Nuclear Theater and move ahead in time with the Future Clock.

Take a video tour of the nuclear power plant.

Excitement, education and entertainment for the whole family are at the Diablo Canyon Nuclear Information Center. And it's all free!

ecology room

Live fish like those in Diablo Cove look back at you as you watch them in the Ecology Room. See for yourself how they live with their new neighbor, the Diablo Canyon Nuclear Power Plant.

The endless pageant of life in the sea, on land and in the sky is halted for a moment here so that you can examine it and imagine yourself a part of it.

See the squirrels, meadow mice, frogs, lizards and other animals and birds that live together with man in this area.

Look past the glass wall to the outdoor world just a step away. Your imagination can fill in the wind, the ocean spray and the coastal fog.

You'll feel more a part of the life around you while you visit the Ecology Room.

the future clock

Walk into the mind-expanding Future Clock, a multi-media slide presentation that thrusts you ten years ahead in time. See how PG&E balances the scale of energy needs today so that you and your family can live comfortably tomorrow.

nuclear theater

You'll think, learn and be entertained in the Nuclear Theater as you watch the story of man's progress from the discovery of fire to nuclear power.

Three screens and stereo sound give you exciting and thoughtful glimpses of Columbus setting out for a new world, the first automobile and the first man on the moon.

Then see how Einstein's theories led to man's control of nuclear fission and the use of this modern, clean fuel in generating electricity to meet the energy requirements of our society.

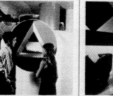

energy and the environment

Individual slide and sound shows explain the nuclear plant's relationship to air quality, radiation and water quality. See how much energy is required to clean up the environment and keep it clean. Turn the crank on the "Low Cost of Power" display to find out the amount of energy needed to generate one cent's worth of electricity.

archaeology

By the time Spanish explorers first saw California, Indians had been living in Diablo Canyon for about 9,000 years.

In thousands of years of progress they hunted, made arrows and spears and invented tools.

Although early Indian life was simple, there was still time for making bowls, ornaments, and even whistles. You'll enjoy this cultural exhibit.

Diablo Canyon Nuclear Information Center pamphlet.

The Atomic Industrial Forum which is a "Public Affairs and Information Program" housed at 7101 Wisconsin Avenue, Washington, D.C., 20014, issues what appear to be "scientific" pamphlets for public education. Among those pertinent to this essay are: *How Nuclear Plants Work; Nuclear Reactor Safety* and *Plutonium in Perspective*. These pamphlets are distributed through many "public" facilities. I picked up my copies at Pacific Gas & Electric Company in San Luis Obispo, the center of the Diablo Canyon controversy. Just a few excerpts from the brochure *Plutonium in Perspective* compared to parallel statements from Dr. Caldicott's essay illustrate the vast differences between official government and public institution language and the alternative, anti-standard positions of those seeking to convey alternative information:

Plutonium in Perspective

Of benefit and risk: Nuclear power plants this year will generate more than 200 billion kilowatt-hours of electricity – enough to meet the needs of about 24 million households. Most of this energy will be produced by the fissioning or splitting of uranium atoms in their fuel, but up to one-third will come from another fissionable element – plutonium – created in the fuel during reactor operation. Not all this material, however, is consumed while producing power. In the fuel rods routinely removed from these reactors over the year, nearly five tons of fissionable plutonium will remain. . . . Putting this resource to work, however, is being delayed by controversy over plutonium, depicted by some as a *new* element: the most hazardous substance known. . . . In fact, many tons of plutonium have been produced, recovered, purified, fabricated, stored and transported for more than 35 years in government, military and research programs. . . . And during this time there has never been known a fatality due to plutonium's toxicity nor a theft for unlawful weaponry. . . Hazards readily controlled: Like most materials, plutonium presents potential risks together with its immense benefits. However these hazards are neither unique nor more difficult to control than those of many other substances routinely handled by industry. . . . But plutonium is not particularly hazardous: it can not harm people it does not reach.

At the Crossroads

. . . You see, the body handles plutonium like iron . . . combines it with the iron transporting proteins, so that it crosses the placenta, the organ that supplies the blood to the developing fetus . . . So if a piece of plutonium lodges in that fetus and kills the cell that is going to make the right half of the brain, the baby will be born deformed. Or if it kills the cell that will make the septum of the heart, the baby will have a hole in its heart. . . . Geneticists say that we probably won't live to see these effects . . . Now, . . . of the elements that come out of the nuclear reactor; iodine 131, strontium 90, cesium 137, and plutonium, . . . the first three elements are . . . beta emitters and plutonium is an alpha. . . . alpha emitters – and plutonium, in particular – are the most carcinogenic or cancer-producing substances we have ever known . . . And plutonium is man-made. It is appropriately named after Pluto, the god of Hell. . . . When miners breathe it into their lungs, they can get lung cancer. In years past, 20 to 50% of uranium miners died of lung cancer. . . . In San Francisco Bay at the Farallon Islands, they have discovered . . . 45,000 55-gallon drums containing plutonium. . . . which were dumped there by the military and a third to a half of them are ruptured and leaking. And that's where they catch their fish for San Francisco.

The "producers of experience" twist fundamental issues such as organic life (the fetus), health and safety at work (the miners and dozens of other examples), and food (plutonium filtering into the fishing waters of San Francisco Bay and West Valley, New York, where there are 600,000 gallons of high-level toxic waste on the brink of leaking into Lake Erie) into economic and technological and military issues.

Arcane philosophies of knowledge understand that the esthetic ritualization of life will provide for the transcendent material experience. Rituals are organized manifesting themselves through sacraments and symbols among which is matrimony (in the company of ordinations, baptisms, rites of passage (confirmation) and drama, architecture, poetry or literature, music, sculptural objects, dance and drawing or painting). It is no accident that contemporary structures continue to maintain these universal human practices while at the same time contouring them to the socio-cultural expression of the historical period in which they are operative. In an age in which the oppressive horrible reality is that life shudders ready to shatter on the brink of the end, nudged along by those with the domination of economics as their master, the luciferian wedlock joins the most powerful structures of contemporary humanity for the purpose of complete destruction.

[1]Max Horkheimer and Theodor W. Adorno, *Dialectic of Enlightenment*, (New York: Herder and Herder), 1969, as quoted from the essay "The Culture Industry: Enlightenment as Mass Deception."
[2]Guy DeBord, *Society of the Spectacle*, (Detroit: Black & Red unauthorized translation) 1970.
[3]Todd Gitlin, *The Whole World Is Watching: The Making and Unmaking of the New Left by The Media*, (Berkeley, The University of California Press) 1980. In this grammar of interaction, Gitlin lists several "framing devices" which aided the media in maintaining its position as ". . . core systems for the distribution and association, symbol and rhetoric, through which ideology becomes mainfest and concrete. . . .: a. trivialization; b. polarization; c. emphasis on internal dissension; d. marginalization; e. disparagement of numbers; and f. disparagement of the movement's effectiveness."
[4]Dr. Helen Caldicott, *At The Crossroads*, (San Francisco: Abalone Alliance) 1979.
[5]Gilles Ivain, "Formula for a New City", *International Situationiste*, No. 1, 1958 as quoted in Christopher Gray's *The Incomplete Work of the Situationist International*, (London: Free Fall Publications), 1974. Gilles Ivain was Ivan Chtcheglov's pen name.
[6]Jean Baudrillard, *For A Critique of the Political Economy of the Sign*, (St. Louis: Telos Press Ltd.), 1981, as quoted from the essay "Requiem for the Media".

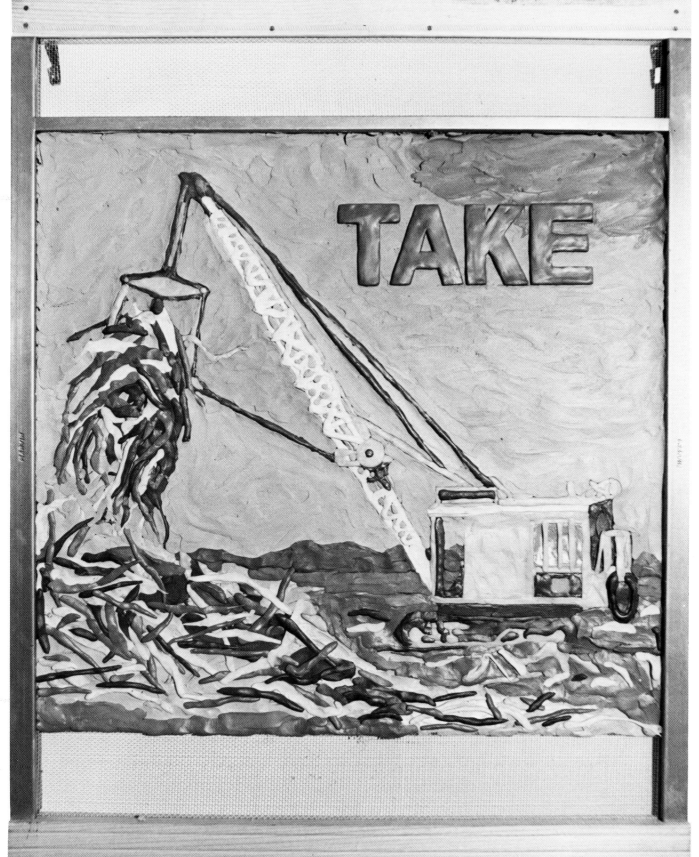

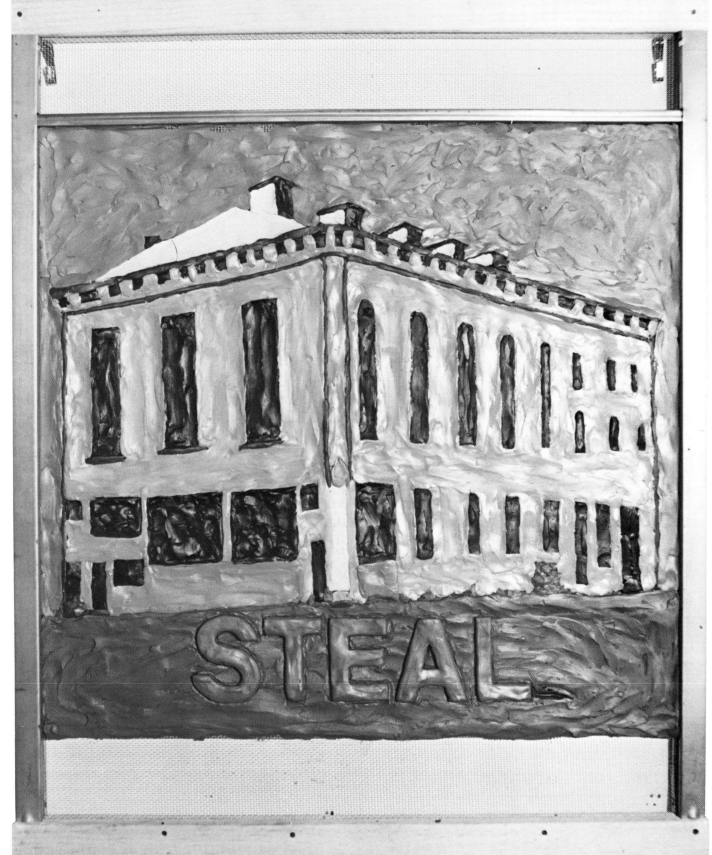

The End of Liberalism (Part II)

Albert Speer, *The Cathedral of Ice*, 1936; NSDAP Rally, Nuremberg, 1936

"The corporation logo is flashing on and off
  in the sky . . .
They got you running to the Night Rally
Night Rally
Night Rally
Night Rally . . ."

Elvis Costello[1]

The essential truth about art of the last 30 years, but continually erased from consciousness by the prevailing ideology of internationalist liberalism, is that Fascism didn't "die" with the cessation of World War II, replaced by *avant garde*, progressive art, but remains the repressed collective unconsciousness of the present. New techniques of mass psychological or product representation, and the propaganda icon (swastika, national flag, corporation logo) replaced traditional forms of representation in Nazi propaganda and spread to post-war corporate advertising. Adorno and Horkheimer in 1944 were already noticing the concurrence between Nazi propaganda and capitalist advertising:

"The Fuhrer('s) . . . voice rises from the street loudspeakers to resemble the howling of sirens arousing panic—from which modern propaganda can scarcely be distinguished anyway. . . .

The system obliges every product to use advertising . . . Advertising becomes art and nothing else, just as Goebbels—with foresight—combines them: *l'art pour l'art*, advertising for its own sake. . . . Advertising and the culture industry merge technically as well as economically. In both cases the same thing can be seen in innumerable places, and the mechanical repetition of the same cultural product has come to be the same as the propaganda slogan. In both cases the insistent demand for effectiveness makes technology into psychotechnology, into a procedure for manipulating men. . . ."
—*Adorno and Horkheimer: Dialectic of Enlightenment*[2]

In the Cold War against Communism, advertising merges with patriotism; the subjective desires of the consumer are enlisted by the ad, coercing him to consume more goods "for a better life." As the product becomes inseparable from the advertising image, the corporate trademark, like Coca Cola, functions as a pychologically all-pervasive archetype.

Bauhaus design is subsumed into corporate technology. It focuses upon the *trademark*, required to individualize (personalize) the corporation, so that the corporation as an identity might exist as another friendly person in democratic society (a "good neighbor"). But, at the same time, the trademark also suggests the universal and totalizing reach of the corporation—its efficacy in the transformation of undifferentiated Nature into progressive technology for Man. Twin influences on corporate design, from identifying logo and "high-tech" graphics are the combination of Bauhaus rationalism and Fascist psychology. Present day "high-tech" design uses both Bauhaus technological allusions and those of Fascist totalitarianism. The light spectacles of Speer linked electric technology with cosmo-mythology-light emanating from the sky giving Hitler's regime an aura of Heaven-sent power. Likewise modern corporate graphics expresses technological might through either the neutral style of rigid formalism or high-tech spectacles of "space-age" gleaming luminescence inspired by Hollywood spectacle and special effects.

Advertising techniques merge with those of large-format color photography and film, placing the spectator in a new relation to the overwhelming voyeuristic image which, as Laura Mulvey observes in "Visual Pleasure and Narrative Cinema", produces "the alienated subject, torn in his imaginary memory by a sense of loss, by the terror of potential lack in (his) phantasy."[3]

The transparent view of "reality" which film gives is the result of technology which has "penetrated so deeply into reality that its [illusion of a] pure aspect . . . of reality (without equipment) . . . [is] the height of artifice" (Walter Benjamin). The film appears to present a view of present-time unfolding without the awareness a theater-goer has of the play's illusion. Film, observed in a darkened room where each spectator sits immobilized as they fix their gaze on a single hypnotic frame of light, semi-somnolent, isolated, but surrounded by the presence of others, produces a pleasure much like that of a dream which can later be discarded and disavowed. Below the conscious level of apparent "reality" which the film presents, there is a subliminal effect on the viewer. Film implants a manufactured "memory", which from then on will function as if it was actually experienced by the spectator's unconscious.

"Triumph of the Will"

Speer's light spectacle was filmed by Leni Riefenstahl in "The Triumph of the Will." With Speer's political architecture of the total spectacle and with Riefenstahl's film-document as total propaganda, the "political becomes aesthetic" (Benjamin). The legitimation of political power becomes inseparably linked to the production of entertainment spectacle.

The architectural relation of theater to the production power through the manipulation of the ruled's sense perceptions is superceded by Hollywood film's depth psychology. A new architecture arises from *mise-en-scene* designed for filmic perception. Architecture begins to become, itself, a form of film.

Much of the impact of "Triumph of the Will" derives from Albert Speer's *mise en scene* for the Rally. Speer's staging of the Rally's spectacle made use of gigantic ban-

Hitler looking at Speer's architectural plans in the architect's atelier, Obersalzberg, spring 1934

ners, powerful searchlights placed at 40-foot intervals and visible at up to 25,000 feet, and an enormous eagle of 100 foot wing span. In Speer's words:

"The feeling was of a vast room, with the beams serving as mighty pillars of infinitely high outer walls. Now and then a cloud moved through this wreath of lights, bringing the elements of surrealistic surprise to the mirage . . . This 'cathedral of light' was the first luminescent architecture."
—Albert Speer, "Oppositions," no. 12

The film begins with a view of various cloud formations through the cockpit of a plane. A pan from right to left emphasizes the dynamic forward thrust of the plane through the clouds.

"The clouds [act as a] lure [for the gaze] into an otherwise empty and infinite space [the sky] while simultaneously signifying the very emptiness and infinity they mask. . . . They . . . signify spectacle itself. . . . The spectating subject is inscribed, via the spectacle of the cloud formations, in interrelationship with an easily flowing and effortless series of movements . . . the gaze able almost to encompass the infinite . . . [with] apparently limitless power."[5]

As the plane descends, "the clouds appear to draw apart like a stage-curtain, to reveal the visual spectacle of the city itself, spread out for our gaze . . . The plane's shadow passes over the street and its parading troops . . . The spectator's gaze (above the crowd, above the city) . . . (is) all encompassing."[6] After Hitler emerges from the plane, a series of shots relates the crowd's gaze and that of the movie-audience's to Hitler as privileged object—Hitler the political 'star'—whom millions can subliminally identify with via film and radio.

"Abstract Expressionism"

In American art Abstract Expressionism emerges as the existential revolt/last stand of the isolated artistic "self" in a climate of conformity and increasing objectification created by mass techniques of social control.

"The unfriendliness of society . . . is difficult for an artist to accept. Freed from a false sense of security and community, the artist can abandon his plastic bankbook, just as he has abandoned other forms of security. Both the sense of community and of security depend on the familar. Free of them, transcendental experience became possible."
—Mark Rothko (1947)

Action Painting proposed a radical subjectivity which plunges the spectator into himself (within the painting's ambiguous, non-objective images). Jeff Wall notes these characteristics of Abstract Expressionism:

" 'Scale and materiality' are new *forms of privacy* . . . (a privacy which) is posed as a public, epic, theatrical issue; the painting becomes an 'event' . . . in which the destruction of modern tradition of rhetoric is enacted. This is blown up to the heroic scale . . . . as [signifier of the] 'heroism' of the 'existential' struggle . . . Shape is the result of the artist's enactment (theatrical re-enactment) of his relation to the primal force of being through undifferentiated gestures."[8]

The irony is that at the same moment that Abstract Expressionism was evolving its oversized, abstractly subjective painting, advertising forms also made a shift, toward the oversized billboard, use of the color photograph, the wide-screen film and the "picture magazine" (*Life, Look*) as formats which "plunged the spectator inside" the giant images. Like the viewer of an Abstract Expressionist painting, the viewer of the new publicity-form inserts himself into a psychologically ambiguous space where the absence of objectively signifying meaning allows the unconscious "self" to project a "personal" meaning. Abstract Expressionism can also be read as the dramatic spectacle of the artist's "self" in relation to the public. This, along with the anxiety of the

artist to make a big impact—despite his avowed disapproval of official culture—fed the media's need for new heroes. *Life* magazine "discovers" the "New American Art" and "a new American genius," Jackson Pollock, whose romantic-tragic life-story provides a native equivalent to that of Van Gogh, as depicted in *Lust for Life.* The espousal of art as self-expression divorced from explicit social content by Abstract Expressionism also allowed it to be quickly assimilated and "Americanized" by the media. Although the artist still believed that the meaning of his work was determined solely by his uncompromised, subjective intuition, market and media forces were, in fact, giving the work a different meaning—a meaning which was beyond the artist's control.

Jasper Johns was the first American artist to fully understand that the newly subjectivized advertising icon and the gestures of the Abstract Expressionist painting (which struggled against the cultural domination of these new forms) were virtually identical. Because Johns' work (and psyche) takes a *passive* position relative to the phenomena, the opposite of Abstract Expressionism's active struggle, the advertising/propaganda icon which invades the unconscious, private space of the individual is now experienced unmediated. Johns' work directly confronts the loss of an undivided "self" with the totalitarianism of mechanical reproduction and a publicity form becoming all-pervasive, determining both popular and fine art forms and meaning. This is the unconscious core "truth" which it is liberalism's ideological task to keep concealed. Liberalism proposes an art of social change or formalist abstraction which psychologically denies this loss of individual self. With Johns, however,

". . . rather than profound art being inherently antagonist to manipulative psychology, propaganda forms of representation become the ground-point of an artistic mode of representation, which abnegates its historical 'right' of composition (and transformation) *apparently* in favor of a quite 'direct' replication of the propaganda form within the frame of the painting."
—Jeff Wall[9]

When Pop Art first appears, it is outright anti-humanist, a *deliberate* reversal of Abstract Expressionism's objections to mechanical reproduction and advertising. This was done in order to demystify the liberalist belief in genius, the artist's unique gesture and the romantic idealism of art:

"The reason I'm painting this way is because I want to be a machine. Whatever I do, and do machine-like, is because it is what I want to do. I think it would be terrific if everybody was alike. . . . Machines have less problems. I'd like to be a machine, wouldn't you?"
—Andy Warhol[10]

Warhol is paraphrasing ideas from a favorite film of his, "The Creation of the Humanoids". Humanoids, robots of advanced design, whose bodies and stocks of knowledge are finally indistinguishable from those of humans, have been programmed to serve the interests of mankind. Although in many cases robots can out-perform and out-think humans and lack the conflicting emotions and cruelty manifested by humans, it is argued by human philosophers that humanoid robots have no soul.

They are treated as slaves by the essentially non-working human race, subjected to occasional acts of brutality by "McCarthyite" persecutions organized by a society of working-people who fear losing their jobs to the robots. These "Human Leaguers," despite their "correct" humanistic views, are shown as like the present-day Ku Klux Klan, fighting against the inevitable and more just and rational new order of the machines. Belief in "humanity," at the expense of the symbiotic relationship of machine and man, is shown to be naive bigotry. There is a silent revolution by the robots, who gradually replace human bodies with machine parts. Before this, humans had been entering into "union" with robots of the opposite sex and through their own choice, electing to convert to robots. As the "Brechtian" style of acting throughout the film, by humans and robots, is coldly neutral and stiff, we are not only "distanced" from human identification (allowed to examine the philosophical/historical consequences of the behavior represented/ actor's behavior), but made to take on the viewpoint of the already dominant robot civilization. Despite our identification with the robot's view, there is still a repressed, bitter-sweet nostalgia for the emotionally based (former) human civilization, doomed to replacement by the stoicism of the new order.

"Outside is the world; it's there. Pop art looks out into the world; it appears to accept its environment, which is not good or bad but different. The heroes depicted in comic books are fascist types, but I don't take them seriously, a political point. I use them for purely formal reasons, and that's not what those heroes were invented for."
—Roy Lichtenstein[11]

In later Pop Art, Johns' sense of psychological terror was replaced by an ambiguous, ironic acceptance, an ironically celebratory "optimism" about the facticity of the new American consumer culture—seen as inevitable. Advertising images are depicted as neutral phenomena, the artist's "self" suppressed behind a "coolly" "realistic" attitude.

Andy Warhol's *Brillo Boxes*

Jasper Johns, *Three Flags*, 1958

Another "distancing" which the later Pop artists employed, which also tended to repress the emotional primacy of the commercial images, was to ironically make the art-object itself into just another packaged product or advertising-like icon. Warhol's Brillo boxes and Lichtenstein's reproduction of printed color comics package themselves, commenting on the already packaged, stereotypical images they reproduce. Pop is a representation of a representation; it represents media's representation, which is in a second-hand, removed relation to "reality." Pop's "new" "realism" does not pretend to represent "reality" directly. Andy Warhol makes *himself* (the self-referential subject of his art) into a self-packaged "star," his production into his own "studio system." Warhol's name becomes mass cultural (propaganda) icon—"trademark"—which allows Warhol's works and image to be consumed on the level of his own celebrity/fame. Partly, Warhol's "acceptance" of mass society is a response to the dilemma of the previous generation of American Abstract Expressionist artists, whose subjective statements had been turned into products and the artist into media-packaged "hero" without his conscious knowledge, in exchange for the work's cultural acceptance through fame and mass distribution via media. Replacing Johns' irony of the "failure of art" with an "art as business" pragmatism (which could, if one wished, but also might not, be interpreted as ironic), Warhol's work accommodates itself to the surface of already represented phenomena. A psychological closure takes place; Warhol's psyche is whatever one wants it to be, a media cliche. Where Jackson Pollock allowed his "genius" to be documented by Hans Namuth's film of his creation of a painting, Warhol took the production of films into his own hands. Undercutting the notion of the "underground" film of films about artists, Warhol made the decision to make films in the Hollywood mode of production and distribution—for a mass audience. This marked a decisive rejection by an avant-garde "gallery" artist of the 19th century tradition of art-for-art's-sake, made in private, in the artist's studio. In the case of Warhol's films, it meant a shift in his role from cameraman/director to producer, and eventually, to executive producer—delegating "creative decisions" to others (including his "stars") in his "Factory's" employ.

"Minimal Art, Film and Architecture"

"Minimal Art," when it first appeared, played with architectural ironies in a manner related to "Pop Art." Flavin's early light "icons" (his term) clearly alluded both to Tatlin's Constructivist "monuments" (also picking up Tatlin's ironic reference to earlier Russian religious icons) and to Speer's Nazi Rally light installations as forerunners of the aesthetics of today's public/commercial lighting system. LeWitt's repetitive, humanly impenetrable cubic grid forms allude, with ironic detachment, to the "dumbness" and the bureaucratic omnipresence of "fascist", corporate-state, post-war architecture.

Buzz Spector has pointed out the close relation between Minimal Art and corporate trademarks and two-dimensional design. Don Judd's vertically stacked or horizontally aligned boxes projecting from the wall maintain a rigidly regulated measure with respect to

"voids between elements, proximity to corners or projecting architectural elements, and distance from boxes to floor . . . these measures are three-dimensional contextual cues to the identity of the works–spaces characteristically 'Judd' . . ."[12]

Similarly the combinations of symbol and type in a typical corporation trademark design, such as that of "Herman Miller," function in terms of explicitly predefined characteristic space intervals between elements, including the spaces between letters.

This is William C. Agee's description of a typical Judd "stack" piece:

"The stacks vary from 5 to 10 units, but their boxes are modular in sizes, always measuring either 9×40×31 inches, or 6 by 4. Intervals between them are 9 inches and 6 inches respectively, for the large and small stacks."[13]

Functionalist architecture produced on a mass-scale by Skidmore, Owings and Merrill, Philip Johnson, etc. after the war became a humanly alienating stereotype. This new, alienating, urban architectural landscape was depicted by filmmakers such as Pasolini and Antonioni. These films were influences on American "Minimalists" such as LeWitt and Morris, as well as on Italian architecture. Aldo Rossi speaks of the impact Italian neo-Realist films had upon his work and of his desire some time to himself turn to films.

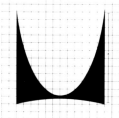

sizes
A = cap height
B = width of "M"
Throughout the manual the terms "symbol" and "logotype" are used in reference to the mark and the words "herman miller" respectively.
The symbol is retained unchanged as an established identifier of Herman Miller. When used with the logotype, which is lower case helvetica medium, the symbol is the same width as the letter "m" in the logotype and is no closer than the distance "A" from the logotype.
When applied as a unit, the symbol and logotype should be no closer than the distance "A" to any border or other elements of typography or design.

"Emergence of Hollywood"

The technical characteristics of the film media, Walter Benjamin hypostulated, have caused the unique "aura" or presence of the actor to be replaced with his superficial characteristics which could be edited into any meaning the director desired by composing "the sequence of positional views." This loss of presence in film was compensated for by the development of an off-screen "buildup of (the actor's) personality." The economics of the film industry were built upon the concept of the "star" for producers discovered that the most effective way of creating product identification for their films was through the name brands of film stars. The star system rationalized consumer demand for brand name product while, at the same time, establishing an easy way to rate, distribute, and promote films; finally, as a by-product, it eliminated all but the major studios who had the cash to invest in promoting a star.

Stars had economic exchange value in terms of the society at large. They could be used to advertise new consumer goods and "life-styles" which the American public aspires to. Stars, getting large salaries, soon became new millionaires and celebrities; for this reason, film producers realized that "launching a star into the upper income brackets put her or him in the national limelight and made Hollywood (as an alternative 'reality') a focal point (of publicity)." Stars, unlike conventional political figures, who might be seen as ruthless and scheming to usurp power, are not seen by the public as objects of envy, but more resembled Greek gods, their foibles and personal tragedies magnified by the press and legend.

The first Renaissance theater organized the perspective of the spectacle on stage so that the ideal spectator came to be the Prince seated in the rear loggia as tangible representation of the power structure. The actors addressed their words to his position (gaze), representing in their stage-play a work reflecting his viewpoint.

Later, kings themselves became actors in royal pageants; they would represent Greek or Roman gods from whom they traced their mythical descent. Their performance over, they might descend from the stage, mingling with the nobility, who had been spectators. With Louis XIV, the king becomes *writer-director and starring actor*, in a drama staged to reinforce an elaborate hierarchy, constructed by the king's play, exactly defining the range of authority and position at court, through dress code and rules of court, etiquette and ritual. Everything "natural", such as eating a meal, was subjected to this artifice. Declaring himself "Sun King," Louis XIV ordained Versailles the "Sun Temple." His ultimate aim was to consolidate national identity and unity, linking the myth of the Absolute Monarch to the spiritual essence of France as Nation.

Hitler, a self-made politician and actor, legitimized his ideology and power through media.

Ronald Reagan is the first professional actor selected by corporate media interests to represent *its* interests to become ruler of a nation.

"President Ronald Reagan"

"On the screen appeared the enormous, three-dimensional full color familiar ruddy but tanned, healthy, hard-cut features of Talbot Yancy . . . The Protector . . . programmed by a computer which in

turn is fed speeches by well-trained elite men (was) in acutality a robot simulacrum. . . Solemnly, at its large desk, with the American flag behind it . . . the competent, fatherly, mature . . . features. . ."[16]

Philip K. Dick's 1967 sci-fi novel, "The Penultimate Truth"[17], depicts a world after World War III, divided into two spheres, a densely populated underground population, and the other an aristocracy living on the earth's surface. Those on the surface manipulate the underworld people via television — programming the pseudo-Yance's speeches to convince people that the earth's surface remains contaminated with fallout. The aristocracy's rationale for their deception is a fear that if the population below rose up, the earth's ecological balance would be destroyed and that another, devastating war could ensue. . .

Ronald Reagan's career began as a Hollywood film "contract player," one of many actors signed by the major studios in the 30's and 40's for movies they produced on an assembly-line-like basis. Studio corporate heads totally controlled their actors, constructing their public images through typecasting them into 'appropriate' publicly consumable roles. Casting an actor determined not only the type of roles they were likely to play for the rest of their contract, how they were represented via media in their "real-life" personalities to the public. In turn, a star's "personality" conditioned the public's identification and unconscious response to media manipulated stereotypes. Reagan was usually cast as the wholesome, athletic, all-American "boy next door." A particularly outstanding role was in the film, "King's Row," where he portrayed a young man injured in an auto crash. Reagan is treated by a doctor, who, prior to the accident, had violently objected to Reagan's dating his daughter. The doctor unnecessarily amputates both of the athletic Reagan's legs. Coming out of the anesthesia, Reagan asks, "Where's the rest of me?"[18]

Reagan's boyish film roles over, he adapted himself to the medium of television, becoming host and occasional star of the TV series, "The General Electric Theater." Reagan had, in the 40's, been active in the Screen Actors' Guild as an anti-communist Democrat. General Electric proposed the actor as their public relations spokesman.

He would travel the banquet circuit to speak about the virtues of the free enterprise system and against government intervention. Paid a large retainer and provided with scripts, Reagan's philosophy accommodated itself easily to his latest role. From actor in a corporate studio system to spokesman for another large corporation Reagan evolved an intimate style better adapted to presentation of self on television. He managed to avoid the pitfalls of Hollywood actors "down on their luck" who appeared on TV in roles in commercials as 'themselves' selling some product. Reagan was always able to project a sense of being completely "himself" — of his complete integrity and belief in his role.

"Not so long ago," he would recount, "two friends of mine were talking to a Cuban refugee. He was a businessman who had escaped from Castro. In the midst of his tale of horrible experiences, one of my friends turned to the other and said, 'We don't know how lucky we are!' The Cuban stopped and said, 'How lucky you are? I had some place to escape to!' And in that sentence he told the entire story. If freedom is lost here there is no place to escape from."[19]

Where Hitler's identity took on new psychological-political dimensions through his use of the film and radio mediums, Reagan's original film persona was redefined through television. Perhaps it was the combination of our familiarity with the Reagan stereotype in films re-played on television in conjunction with his "non-political" political status which built his new image. (In this, he resembles General Dwight Eisenhower, whose fame was initially established in an arena "above" politics, therefore whose integrity was unassailable, and who, like Reagan, was perceived as a "nice guy.")

1 Costello, Elvis, "Night Rally," written by Elvis Costello, 1978
2 Adorno, Theodor and Horkheimer, "Dialectic of Enlightenment"
3 Mulvey, Laura, "Visual Pleasure and Narrative Cinema," *Screen*, Autumn, 1975
4 Speer, Albert interviewed by Dal Co, Francesco and Polano, Segio, *Opposition*, Spring, 1978: 12
5 Neale, Stephen, "Documentary and Spectacle," *Screen*, Spring, 1979
6 *Ibid*, Rothko, Mark, 1947, quoted by Wall, Jeff, "Problems," unpublished
7 Wall, Jeff, "Problems," unpublished, Vancouver, B.C., 1980
8 *Ibid*
9 *Ibid*
10 Warhol, Andy, quoted in the Warhol exhibition catalogue, Moderna Museet, Stockholm, Sweden, 1968
11 Lichtenstein, Roy, interviewed by Swenson, Gene, "*Art News*," November, 1965
12 Spector, Buzz, "Objects and Logotypes: Relationships Between Minimalist Art and Corporate Design," The Renaissance Society at the University of Chicago, 1980
13 Agee, William C. (quoted by Spector), "Unit, Series, Site: A Judd Lexicon," Art in America, 63, 3 (May-June, 1975): 40-49
14 Benjamin, Walter, "The Work of Art in the Age of Mechanical Reproduction"
15 Benjamin, Walter, *Op. cit.*
16 Mitchel, George, "The consolidation of the American Film Industry 1915-1920," *Cine-Tracts*, Spring, 1979
If stars lost stature, their "star" status was always potentially recoverable. As the public felt that it was *their* desire which had made them "stars," the public resented the producers' unfair power over the "stars' lives; it never realized that it was the producer who had created the illusion of "stardom" in the first place, which they, the public, believed in.
17 Dick, Phillip K., "The Penultimate Truth," 1967
18 The title of Reagan's 1950 autobiography was, "The Rest of Me."
19 Reagan, Ronald, quoted in Smith, Hedrich, Clymer, A., Silk, L., Lindsy, R. and Burt, R., "Reagan The Man, The President," Macmillan, 1980

3 DRUGS
ABUSED BY AMERICANS
A New Video Tape

Caffeine

Nicotine

Gasoline

GUN CONTROL

BUY IT

BUY IT

THE TIME-BASED CONCEPT OF HIGH TECHNOLOGY IS TRANSFORMING OUR LIFESTYLES. THE CULTURE OF HIGH TECHNOLOGY IS TIMELESSNESS. WE ARE ALL GOING THROUGH A TRANSITION. THE CONCEPT OF TIMELESSNESS MANIFESTS ITSELF IN OUR VALUESYSTEM. I.E. OUR CULTURE. "TIMELESSNESS" OPPOSED TO "VALUABLE AT ALL TIMES" GO TOGETHER FIRST IN THE HIGH TECHNOLOGY AGE. I GUESS THAT'S WHAT ART IS ABOUT.

the following text is part of a telephone interview given by dr. leland seely, general manager of AMI, whom i met per chance on the train from linz to graz.

Richard Kriesche

The Partners

American Microsystems, Inc. headquartered in Santa Clara, California is the semiconductor industry leader in the design and manufacture of custom metal-oxide-silicon large-scale integrated (MOS/LSI) circuits. The company has produced more than 1500 custom MOS/LSI circuits since 1966. It manufactures special circuits for the leading computer manufacturers, telecommunications companies, automobile manufacturers and consumer product companies worldwide. American Microsystems Inc., sales in 1980 were $130 million.

Voest-Alpine AG headquartered in Linz, Austria is the leading industrial organization in Austria, with more than $4 billion in sales by all divisions. The company is a leading steel producer, heavy equipment manufacturer and supplier of complete factories for the production of basic metals, materials and chemicals. Voest-Alpine employs more than 80,000 people in 130 countries worldwide.

RICHARD: the faster the microcomputer works, the better it is.
LEE: yes, that's usually the case.
RICHARD: the more time you take out of the microcomputer, the better it is. so finally you have no time in your microcomputer.
LEE: okay, yes, that's a way of looking at it.
RICHARD: for representing its timelessness AMI is moving into a building which is valid at all times.

The Castle

LEE: we didn't set out purposely to find a castle. we had all of these criteria for locating a plantsite, that didn't specifically say: "hey, we need a castle!" when we found something that satisfied all of these criteria, then it was a castle, associated with the property. so we now had to make a decision with these things in mind. a lot of things that you have mentioned entered into the evaluation of this castle.

i believe that the castle could serve as a very nice trademark or a logo.

i think the idea of contrast went through our mind when we looked at the castle. there is the old valuable building and right next to it would be the high technology modern building. we felt this contrast was a valuable aspect of the castle.

The Fortification

RICHARD: i try to figure out the common ideas between the castle and the high technology, instead of their contrast. castles in their time had been part of the security system. you know, when the invaders came in, people moved into the castle. from there they fought against the invaders. this was one of the functions of the castles. on page seven of your information booklet on AMI you are saying: "the AMI factory in graz, austria occupies 20 hectares (50 acres) and has 10,000 square meters of floor space. to protect customer proprietary circuit design, a full security system limits access into and within the plant and its design area. . ." where you were talking of contrast there seems to me to be no contrast. the castle fits perfect as ideology into what you are doing with AMI.

LEE: symbolizing the security of proprietary information as opposed to the physical security of the inhabitants.

RICHARD: the castle creates security by having a security system. the castle is the ideological background for your own security system.

LEE: resetting the function of the castle into the new high technology age, taking it out of the past may find more common things where we looked to contrast them.

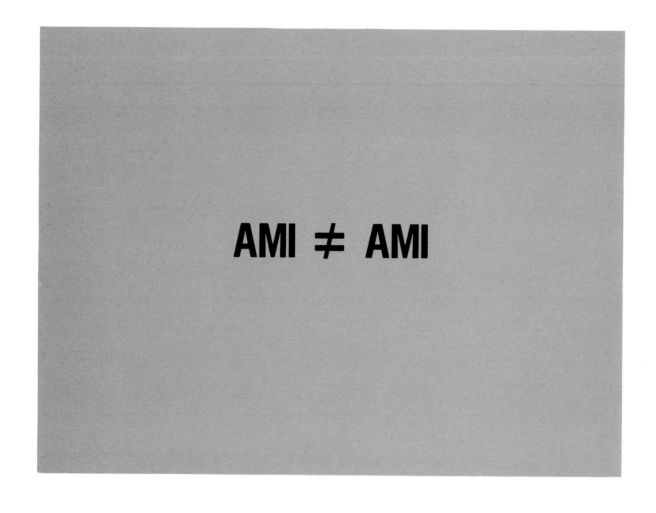

AMI ≠ AMI

LEE: you picked out one, the security function. i should ask you what others did you see in common?
RICHARD: you call yourself AMERICAN MICROSYSTEMS INCORPORATED. in austria you call yourself AUSTRIAN MICROSYSTEMS INTERNATIONAL. AMI is AMI.
LEE: let me just make sure that you have factually what we did there. we set out to maintain the AMI logo. we want that our european customers associate the same people and the same company, that they always have, but with expanded capability as a result of the facilities that we are putting in europe. at the same time we have to make some changes, because here we are now in europe and this company is specifically here to serve the european market. so we don't want to lose the customers that we have got, by becoming unfamiliar to them, and at the same time we want to bring them further along, telling that we have made some changes, that we are here in europe, that we are specifically set up to serve the european market now. so the AMI was certainly intentional. we spent quite some time to come up with: "how do we get an AMI in europe?"
RICHARD: in a way all is part of the representation of AMI.
LEE: absolutely yes.
RICHARD: i made two other versions of AMI. (1) AUSTRIAN MEDIEVAL INSTITUTION and (2) AMERICAN MIND INVASION.
LEE: i love that one. there is more truth to that one than you might think.

AMI TIME INVASION

RICHARD: what do you think about the castle as (1) "AMI—austrian medieval institution"
(2) "AMI—american mind invasion"?
LEE: certainly go together. the castle would symbolize both for us. you talked about putting high technology into the castle. we are certainly invading the mind of the european. yet, dramatically makes the point that we have to make cultural bridges. in fact in the architectural design we have a bridge between the high tech building and the castle. we did it for a more practical reason that we want truck access to the back door of the castle. the new building has a passage way connecting its first floor to that of the castle. so we are physically bridging from high technology building to our castle. that would be certainly symbolic of bridging the cultural differences connnecting the timeless valued building on into our new high technology building.
and i guess ART and the ACTUAL RUNNING OF THE FACTORY and forming the culture of the company here is going to be important. it would certainly be easier to get messages across in artform than just in straight sterile pages of this is what we do.

Seeing double

Advertising ensures that underlying the illusion of choice created by the spectacle of rivalry between manufacturers there is established an involuntary belief that competitive consumption and personal fulfillment are inseparable. The primary unit of consumption is the family, and the administration of high levels of household consumption has fallen to women. It has been estimated that the value of the unpaid labour of housewives is equivalent to a quarter of the gross national product. The collusion of women in their wholesale recruitment as domestic slaves is effected through the unquestioned assumption of a feminine 'domesticity' as natural to them as their biological gender: thus the ubiquitous 'homemaker', apotheosis of feminine virtue and self-fulfillment – an imago to which advertisers hypocritically defer as if it were the ringmaster in their circus of commodities, and not one of their clowns.

Pennis from heaven
Amongst the military vehicles and armour
which line the route to the refreshment marquee,
buyers from third-world countries
congregate around the rocket-launchers.
The production of such goods
provides essential employment, saving many from poverty;
it gives free rein to invention,
and gives the consumer a choice.

Police-of-mind
Several times, military power passed
into the hands of the soldiers.
The soldiers wavered.
A few hours after they had disposed
of a hated superior
they released the others,
entered into negotiations with
the authorities,
and then had themselves shot.

Omnimpotence

Economically speaking, the father's authority in the home is an anachronism which recalls pre-industrial times when he directed family-based production. In most cases today the father is himself merely a commodity in the labour-market. His 'authority' now serves to reproduce in his children his own subservience to corporate and state power, providing them with the image of an ultimately benevolent controlling wisdom through which they will later tend to view all others who wield power over them. The objective authority of the father has collapsed into that gap which the factory opened between work and family-life. Simultaneously master-of-the-house and a servant in his place of employment, the identity of the patriarch as wage-slave is in perpetual transit between work and home.

Flights of fancy
Inessa Armand wanted to write a book about free love.
Lenin wrote her a letter. It concluded:
The issue is not what you subjectively want it to mean,
the issue is the objective logic of class relations
in matters of love.
Shklovsky reminisced: We slept with many of them —
mechanically, the way a man planes boards.

Framed

A dark-haired woman in her late-fifties
hands over a photograph showing the haircut
she wants duplicating 'exactly.'
The picture shows a very young woman
with blond hair cut extremely short.
The hairdresser props it by the mirror

in which he can see the face of his client
watching her own reflection.
When he has finished he removes the cotton cape
from the woman's shoulders. 'That's it', he says.
But the woman continues sitting, continues staring
at her reflection in the mirror.

The vaguest little longing. . .just a yen, really. . .a sense of anticipation. . .a flight of fantasy. . .some small inner awakening. . .a fluttery hope for your wildest dreams. . . That momentary twinge of. . .is it guilt?. . .that holds its own naughty thrill. And then. . .the elation that follows. Something unattainable suddenly attained. Mine! Is it really so dreadful to say it? After all, the thought is there and yes it is. . .smug. . .the sense of possession . . .of ownership of something that is absolutely, definitely, finally perfect. Something you searched for and found and acquired. And every time you gaze up on it you feel radiant, exuberant, and content. When you feel those acqusitive urges. . .the ones that can only be satiated by a financial transaction. . .and the climax of possession. . .

Why not move up-market to a creative shopping experience? Why not commemorate your possessive urges with souvenirs of your shopping excursions and trophies of your acquisitive safaris? And there is only one place to find them. One place in all the world. And that is the Boutique of the 1984 Miss General Idea Pavillion. Browse through our catalogue and then shop in person. . .or use our convenient phone and mail-order service. . .unleash your buying power at the 1984 Miss General Idea Pavillion.

IDEA's

...rda at the Miss General Idea Boutique at the Carmen Lamanna Gallery

BOUTIQUE

ATLANTA
Discover magnificent Peachtree Center, 15 minutes from Atlanta International Airport.

COLUMBUS
Downtown at Ohio Center, near State Capitol, Ohio State University.

INDIANAPOLIS
Hyatt is downtown across from the Convention Center and State Capitol.

KANSAS CITY
At Crown Center, Hyatt has health club, tennis courts, pool.

PHOENIX
Stay at Hyatt across from Phoenix Civic Plaza and Convention Center.

Market fresh vegetables are standard in every Hyatt restaurant. All our vegetable dishes and crisp, colorful garnishes are prepared only from the season's freshest. It's called a touch of Hyatt™.

Other hotels try to give you a touch of Hyatt, but only Hyatt gives you them all. It's this basis for comparison that means you get your money's worth.

Capture the Hyatt spirit at 97 hotels worldwide. For reservations, call your travel planner or 800 228 9000.

A touch of Hyatt

HYATT ⏣ HOTELS

© 1981 Hyatt Corp.

Power and Sentimentality = Asparagus and Chrysanthemums

The practice of advertising—whether in the form of image/texts or corporate architecture—is a preeminent visual and conceptual force in defining the parameters of contemporary mass culture. The task of demystifying its impact upon human perception and behavior and to analyze its mythical implications is a critical issue among many artists and thinkers working today. In comparing contemporary western culture with that of the ancient Greeks, the late theologian Paul Tillich had these comments:

Human existence under the predominance of space is tragic. Greek tragedy and philosophy knew about this. They knew that the Olympic gods were gods of space, one beside the other. Even Zeus was only the first of many equals, and hence subject, together with man and the other gods, to the tragic law of genesis and decay. Greek tragedy, philosophy, and art were wrestling with the tragic law of our spatial existence. They were seeking for an immovable being beyond the circle of genesis and decay, greatness and self-destruction, something beyond tragedy...

It is understandable that finally the Greek mind tried to escape the tragic circle of genesis and decay by escaping reality completely. It is understandable that the last task of Greek philosophy was mysticism ... So we have to ask: What about time and space in mysticism? The answer is: Mysticism is no real escape from the predominance of space. It extinguishes time and space, but in doing so, it maintains the basic presumption that time cannot create something entirely new. ...[1]

The manipulation of the image/text, implicit in the force of most commercial advertising, allows the imprint of a corporate ideology to exist as a fixed insignia upon the mind. By removing the possibility of heightened cognition from the semiotic construct, and thereby establishing the referent (product-symbol) as a tautology capable of disavowing all but its own contextuality, corporate advertising may absolve itself from history and ignore the reality of tragic events. As in the circumstance of Hellenic mysticism, or—for that matter—the *pittura metafisica* of De Chirico,[2] the presence of history is forfeited by a mythical illusion, what Tillich has called "the predominance of space."

In the everyday world of corporate advertising, the function of space occurs on both a surface and a metaphorical level. The message contained within this bipartite structure carries its own authority, an absolute authority founded upon myth.

Much of the highly sophisticated advertising that appears on television or in commercial magazines—regardless of how "cool" or detached the information is presented—relies heavily upon metaphors of sentimentality and power: two thematic concerns which are found in the Greek tragedies of Euripides or Aeschylus, among others. In the contemporary genre, however, these metaphors are derived from images which are common fare in upper middle class culture, usually revolving around either social prestige, glamour, sexuality, or economic idioms. The image/text manipulation not only reflects a formalized set of cultural signs, it also attempts to reify an ideological position in reference to them.

Advertising functions as a carefully integrated formal system in which signs of sentimentality and power are literally *incorporated* into the package. The appeal is frequently made through the use of bold copy or aggressive imagery suggestive of upper middle class fantasies while at the same time

← This ad appeared in the TWA Ambassador *(July 1981) during the month that the Hyatt disaster occurred in Kansas City. The visual appeal of the green asparagus stalks is an effective formal device and a curious choice of subject matter. The presentation of these vertical "spears" carries an aggressive connotation. Also, the relationship of the* raw *to the* cooked *asparagus is particularly suggestive of the symbols used by Levi-Strauss to distinguish between natural and cultural systems.* Whereas the raw asparagus pervades the visual field, the* cooked *asparagus appears on an oval plate and is set within a small photographic insert. However unintentional, the image/text carries an aura of indomitability, paternalism (with sexual overtones), and harsh intimacy. The phrase—"A touch of Hyatt"—implies magic as well as thoughtfulness, power as well as sentimentality. Every detail is guaranteed secure.*

*Claude Levi-Strauss, The Raw and the Cooked. *trans. John and Doreen Weightman (New York: Harper and Row, 1964)*

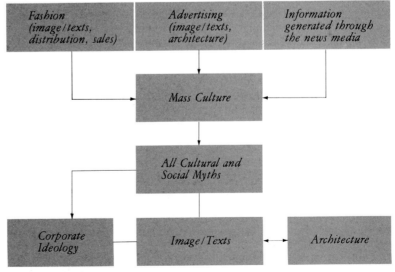

Diagram of information input
to construct image/text

playing upon these psychological insecurities. The bold image/text is contrived in such a way so as to influence the reader's lifestyle and self-concept and thereby to effect decision-making processes in choosing one product over another. Advertising practices of this nature imply stability (in relation to a corporate image) while they are usually less than overt in expressing their proselytizing motives.

The image/text which is adapted to commercial advertising is essentially a product-in-itself. It is a tautology, a convolution of speech, a metonym which projects itself symbolically and in reference to another product: the commodity, the service, the accommodation, the political belief. Most sophisticated advertising not only reflects the ideological concerns of its corporate sponsor, but draws upon accepted myths in popular or mass culture as a means of supporting ideology.

In his book, *Mythologies* (1957), Roland Barthes proposes that the language of myths in contemporary western culture is, in fact, a "metalanguage" which functions in-between the denotative and connotative operations of speech.[3] This metalanguage is useful when applied to the analysis of the image/text in advertising. By analyzing the mechanics of a graphic layout, initially in terms of its denotative function, the reader is then given two essential routes of interpretation. The reference of meaning may be understood specifically (in relation to the product and its ideology) or it may be given a more general syntax of explication, i.e., one in which the myth is extracted which lends credence and support to the ideology. The reference of meaning towards the extraction of the myth is "its total term, or global sign."[4]

According to Barthes, the structure of the supporting myth constitutes a "second-order semiological system" which is formed by "the associative total of a concept and an image."[5] Hence, the corporate infrastructure (ideology) may be read as a composite of signs (the visual code or formal system) reified within the image/text and expressed in relation to

an anonymous recipient in mass culture who is presumably tolerant of the normative myth.

The average reader of a particular magazine is targeted to "consume" the message of the image/text, rather than to examine its form and context as a semiotic system. Elaborate and expensive graphic layouts may attempt to conceal their coding devices, to make their mechanics nearly invisible. The emphasis is directed toward quick perception and easy assimilation of the message. Visual associations, or metonyms, are used regularly in advertising as indirect channels to incite memory recall. Hence, the accompanying product-symbol, i.e. the image photographed in reference to the product is as crucial to the message as the product being advertised. A good advertisement not only strives to sell a product, it tries to sell an attitude toward the product as well.

Although some effective advertising will divert attention from the "bottom line" concerns of its corporate sponsor, the fact remains that the formal specifications of the image/text are bound in their signification to the product. Consequently, the force behind advertising does not represent the reality of everyday life; it represents a myth about contemporary living that is expedient to the product. To succeed, an advertisement has to mystify the spectator. This mystification process depends largely upon a lack of certainty within the social structure as a peculiar optimism in relation to the identity of the self.[6]

The myths which sustain much corporate ideology as reflected in the current uses of advertising are based on social science, not on the aesthetic enrichment of life. Although the image/text may suggest the opposite, the information is generally based on consumer motivation research derived from vapidly contrived polling techniques and statistics.[7] Large-scale advertising of corporate products is conceived in relation to a quantitative support system and calculated by the "fashion" industry. It is a system which tends to co-opt qualitative judgements which challenge normative myths. Finally, it

is a means readily available for asserting a positive profile, regardless of what might be construed as "negative" publicity by the press, especially in a time of tragedy associated with the company name.

The Kansas City Hyatt Disaster

The proposal to build a Hyatt Regency in downtown Kansas City was officially announced at a St. Patrick's Day luncheon in 1973 by the President of Hallmark Cards.[8] Believing that the hotel would enhance the city's reputation as an international convention center, the Chamber of Commerce enthusiastically endorsed the project. Hallmark Cards—the highly successful hometown corporation that once proclaimed itself "an art gallery for the masses"—proved a likely sponsor for such an undertaking.[9] Not only would the new sponsor enhance the city's reputation, it would add a further development to Hallmark's spacious 85-acre Crown Center—"a city within a city" which served as a major tourist attraction and downtown shopping center.

The actual construction of the 43 story, 700 + room complex began in March 1978 and was completed 28 months later. Though slightly modest in comparison with Chicago's O'Hare Hyatt, the spectacular atrium and lobby area became another visual extravaganza. The Kansas City version included an indoor park with terraced flower beds (modeled after the Galleria in Milan), a cascading waterfall, and a canopied glass skylight. Another feature was a series of three "sky bridges" which spanned the atrium at three different levels. These steel-reinforced walkways were held in place by thin steel rods which ran vertically to the ceiling and by riveted steel plates which adhered to the support beams at either end. The use of additional support columns was apparently discouraged lest they intrude upon the ethereal look of the adjacent garden.[10]

On July 17, 1981—approximately one year after the hotel had been inaugurated—the fourth floor walkway tore loose from its rods and collapsed on top of the

The Hyatt tragedy

This is a section of a page from The Kansas City Star *(Sunday, July 19, 1981). Photo:* The Kansas City Times

second story structure directly underneath. The two bridges— both carrying pedestrians at the time—crashed into the lobby where a crowd of some 1,500 people had gathered for an evening Tea Dance.[11] Initial reports estimated 45 persons had been killed—most of them crushed instantly beneath the fallen wreckage. Another 145 persons were reported injured, hurt, or maimed by flying shards of glass and heavy debris.[12] Volunteer rescue workers, medical personnel, foremen, and police worked a constant shift through the night and into the next day pulling victims out from the wreckage. By Satur-

day (July 18), the casualties had risen to 111 as more people were discovered crushed beneath the lower level walkway.[13] The official toll, announced several days later, came to 113 people dead, 186 people injured—some with cuts and bruises, others severely disabled.[14]

Despite the expressed grievances of individual spokesmen, the Hyatt and Hallmark Corporations chose to keep a "low profile" in relation to the press, yet at the same time to maintain a positive image through their own public relations and advertising. The primary task was to get the hotel repaired, reopened, and function-

ing again as normal, and to avoid the tremendous losses in overhead costs.[15] Remarkably, by October 1st—less than 2½ months after the fatal accident—the Kansas City Hyatt announced its renovated interior. The fourth floor walkway was replaced by an extended terrace with steel-reinforced concrete poured to the bedrock. The hotel had reopened just in time for the fall convention season. Rooms gradually began to fill. Full-page ads appeared in various magazines acknowledging the Kansas City Hyatt, garnished with asparagus and chrysanthemums.[16]

61   Robert Morgan

Summary

Advertising in the form of image/texts and architecture with its propensity for spatial function are two manifestations of corporate ideology. They each have the potential to embody myths of sentimentality and power. Yet there is a crucial distinction between the two. Whereas the image/text is contained with a formal system, the formal system of a building complex is always subject to the constraints of "real time" utility. Whereas the power of the myth in a television or magazine ad is psychological and momentary, the power of the myth in the appearance and function of architecture takes on a more far-reaching historical significance. This is not to say that one form is any less pervasive than the other in terms of its cultural influence.

Regardless of their ideological grounds, the parallels between image/texts and architecture have revealed themselves in various manifestations throughout history. Erwin Panofsky regards the construction of Gothic cathedrals as a direct manifestation of the emerging dialectical concerns within the writings of Scholasticists, such as Thomas Aquinas.[17] In this instance, the case could be made that the embodiment of sentimentality and power (the authority of the Church) again prevailed. Because architecture was considered in previous eras the apogee of artistic expression, it maintained a certain status in synthesizing various components within society. Yet today it would seem the accelerated use of advertising media has usurped the status once given to architecture. Few buildings are constructed in the present era which are able to lend positive reification to the social environment in which corporations are so deeply involved. In other words, the human symbolic function in these buildings is missing.[18] Instead, the construction of large corporate complexes, such as Crown Center, or sprawling governmental centers in some of the leading states are generally based on the lowest common denominators—cost efficiency and an uninspired cosmetic appearance.

There is a clear problem in concentrating too much of the societal myth in terms of the image/text and not enough in the structural/symbolic planning of architecture. In spite of the efficient and expedient velocity of the former, to overload its significance for immediate commercial or political effect at the expense of more qualitatively based architecture (read: *social symbolic manifestation*) is to ignore the reality of history in favor of mysticism. While the image/text may serve as a direct legitimation of ideology as generated through the myth of the corporate image, architecture represents the more direct embodiment of social values as perceived in time and space. Buildings are not forgotten so easily as advertising jingles. For any corporation to neglect the responsibility of safety in architecture or the potential mobility and psychological stability of its inhabitants is to deny the importance of the larger social fabric as the very cause of its existence. In so doing, the vulnerability of the image/text as a vehicle for the corporate image becomes an escape device, rather than a positive motion forward.

[1] Paul Tillich, *Theology of Culture*, edited by Robert C. Kimball (New York: Oxford University Press, 1968); pp. 33-35.
[2] It occurred to the author while viewing the "metaphysical paintings" of Giorgio De Chirico recently at the Museum of Modern Art, New York, that "the predominance of space" is the critical factor in the painter's dream-world hypotheses. The sharp orthogonals, the harsh light, the broken columns, and frozen solitary figures have little in reference to history. De Chirico is, indeed, giving us a visual tautology; the projections are constantly inward. The oppressive of his piazzas, arcades, and rooms has much in common with Piranesi; the myth has been sealed. The sense of tragedy cannot be preceived as real, only as another parameter within the confines of space.
[3] Roland Barthes, *Mythologies*. trans. Annette Lavers (New York: Hill and Wang, 1957); pp. 111-117; also see Victor Burgin, "Photographic Practice and Art Theory" in *Two Essays on Art Photography and Semiotics* (London: Robert Self Publications, 1976); pp. 11-12.
[5] *Ibid.*
[6] For a more developed discussion of these issues, see: Erving Goffman, *The Presentation of Self in Everyday Life* (Garden City, NY: Doubleday Anchor Books, 1959).
[7] Marshall McLuhan, *Understanding Media: The Extensions of Man* (New York: A Signet Book, New American Library, 1964); pp. 201-207.

[8] Jeff Coplon, "Did Hallmark Care Enough To Build The Very Best? A Report on the Kansas City Hyatt Tragedy," *Village Voice*, Vo. XXVII, No. 7 (February 10-16, 1982), p. 14.
[9] *Ibid.*, p. 15.
[10] *Ibid.*, p. 15-16.
[11] *The New York Times* (July 18, 1981), front page story.
[12] These figures were reported initially in *The Kansas City Times* (July 18, 1981), front page story.
[13] *The Kansas City Star* (Sunday Edition, July 19, 1981), Special Section, pp. 1-10 HR.
[14] Coplon, *op. cit.*, p. 13.
[15] *Ibid.*, p. 18.
[16] The *United Mainliner* repeated the asparagus ad, while the *TWA Ambassador* used chrysanthemums. Both magazines appeared in October, 1981, the month the Kansas City Hyatt reopened, and both ads cited the hotel along with four other Hyatts. In addition to United and TWA, other airline magazines regularly run Hyatt ads as well.
[17] Erwin Panofsky, *Gothic Architecture and Scholasticism* (New York: A Meridian Book, New American Library, 1957)
[18] Lewis Mumford has suggested that mechanical function and symbolic function are two different aspects of a building in his lecture, "Symbol and Function in Architecture" in *Art and Technics* (New York: Columbia University Press, 1952); pp. 111-135.

This ad appeared in the TWA Ambas- →
sador *(October 1981), the month that the Kansas City Hyatt reopened for business. The same format of the earlier ad is used, whereby an insert photograph echoes the theme of the larger image on a more intimate scale. However, the subject matter has changed from asparagus ("Market fresh vegetables") to chrysanthemums ("the language of fresh flowers"). Although the image of flowers may appear neutral, the saturation of color—bright yellow—is clearly aggressive to the eye. The oval shape of the key-fab, shown within the photographic insert, is consistent with the oval plate shown in the asparagus ad. The glass of wine in the upper right corner of the insert is also consistent with the former ad, except that it has changed from white to rose. The insert reinforces the visual field as both a formal and mythical agent. It suggests intimacy, elegance, and prestige. In Japan, the sixteen-petaled chrysanthemum is the emblem of Imperial Sovereignty. More appropriate to the context: "It gladdens the heart in the season of autumn."**

*Henry P. Bowie, On the Laws of Japanese Painting *(New York: Dover Publications, 1952), pp. 71-72.*

It would be interesting, a few decades from now, to look back at the image the press gives today of the computer, when it has become totally integrated into our life, just as the car, the fridge or the central heating.

What king of image of the computer do periodicals and publicity mean to give ? Here are a few extracts selected out of the professional and non-professional press. The attempts made by the publicity to promote this image are contradictory and such approaches will certainly not be favoured by firms when the mysteriousness of a new technology has vanished.

The images and publicity presented are typical of a constantly recurring set.

1) It has been impossible to find in the promotional image of the memory machines, a technician who is paunchy. It looks as if the beauty of the machine was bound by contract to the beauty of the user. The world of computers is clean, the figure of the programmer, man or woman, must be stylised just as the design of chairs and tables must be the latest.

2) A whole chapter could be written about seduction in relation
with the publicity on the machines which can "revolutionize"
office work or secretarial work. The image of the woman, always
young, always beautiful, charmed by and admiring the machine as
if facing a seductor. Words that come more often are : logic,
intelligence, speediness and power, the foremost qualities of a
superior being.

(3)

(4)

3) In this image which is meant to be given of small computers competent for miscellaneous tasks, specially those for text treatment, care is taken to reassure from a traditional point of view. The vision of the world remains the same : the pyramidal structure of the picture proves it : the chief at the top (the man) set at a place from where he dominates all his department, the subordinates (the women) receiving the orders and executing the work.

4) This is the most megalomaniac picture I could find : the transformation of a new moral order through the computer, a (monotheist) religion in a world (an island) ruled by the programmer, from city life down to organized leisures.

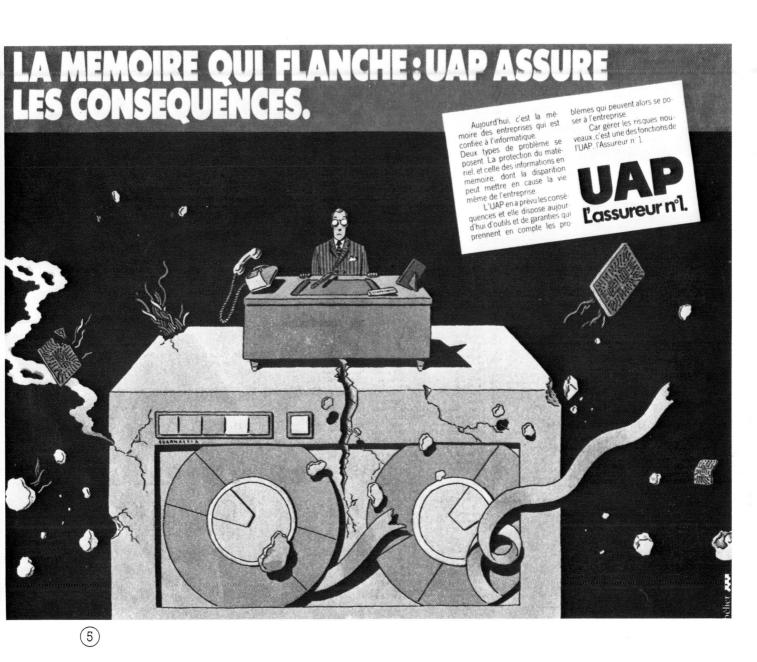

⑤

5) The only negative image of the set. It occurs very seldom but does corroborate all the others ab absurdo. The Indurance Company commits itself to guarantee the material of the company's memory bank since some firms woul be condemned to disappear, should their memory be erased. The picture of the destruction of the computer in the space is not meant to scare the company directors but to convince them to take an insurance against risks of modern times : the misdirection of the information, perhaps the destruction by saborage. It comes to telle us this : there is but one step from beauty and order to chaos∎

Gay-Identified Advertising: The Poppers Industry

Phase 1: 1976, The Advocate. © Pacific Western Distributing Corporation

Definition

Poppers: Butyl or isobutyl nitrite compounds. Marketed under several brand names: Rush, Bolt, Locker Room, Natural Brute, Cum, Hi Ball, Hard Ware, Quick Silver. Packaged in small vials or ampules, available by mail order, retailed in adult bookstores, gay bathhouses, drug paraphernalia shops. Commonly used by gay men as an inhalant for hedonistic purposes, especially during intercourse for the prevention of premature ejaculation and for the relaxing of the anal sphincter muscle.

Production

With an estimated gross revenue of $50 million per year, production of butyl nitrite compounds (i.e. poppers) comprises the most lucrative business enterprise in the gay world.[1] Despite evidence suggesting a link between poppers and gay-related immune deficiency diseases, as well as consumer studies that have identified carcinogenic properties in nitrites, poppers usage remains a prominent feature of gay life.[2]

The absence of restriction or control, and the relative ease with which the substance can be produced, made poppers a profitable, small overhead business during the 1970's. By the middle of the decade, more ambitious manufacturers, anticipating the commercial potential in quantity production, entered the market. The best known and most profitable of these concerns, Pharmex, Ltd./Pacific Western Distributing Corp., advertises itself as "the world's largest manufacturer of liquid incense."[3]

Although both the medical field and government agencies are aware of the fact that poppers are invariably used as an inhalant (i.e. drug), manufacturers have avoided any form of federal drug control or regulation by labelling the product as a liquid incense or room odorizer.

Phase 2: 1980, Drummer Magazine, © Pacific Western Distributing Corporation

Promotion: Pharmex, Ltd.

When Pharmex, Ltd. first marketed Rush in 1976, the poppers industry was dominated by small concerns whose advertising strategies were based on a macho, leather-styled consumer image. Locker Room, the best known product at that time, was merchandised as "an aroma of men." Other brands traded equally on a kind of hot and heavy backroom sex image. In contrast, Pharmex, Ltd. developed the packaging and promotion of Rush with an identification strategy geared to a young, more mainstream-identified gay male population.

A. Presentation:

The packaging of Rush, in small yellow vials or ampules with red graphics, imbues the product with a slick, modern image—distinct from the medicinal look generated by the brown glass vials employed by most manufacturers. The choice of the name Rush, while descriptive of the product's effect and metaphorically sexual, avoids the direct pornographic references common to other brands. Packaging and identification not only made Rush unique when it was first introduced, but distinguished it from the illicit, bootleg image fostered by other poppers producers.

In its six year history, Pharmex, Ltd. has developed three distinct promotional campaigns for Rush. Each phase has served to reinforce Rush's identification with the mainstream gay consumer.

B. Phase 1:

Rush's first advertisements appeared as cartoon-style graphics. Superman, Captain Marvel and other comic book heroes were shown zapping villains with a bottle of Rush in hand. Each of these advertisements was accompanied by the slogan "Purity, Power, Potency." These advertisements traded on the nostalgic potential of the cartoon character and used the comic book "hero" as a strategy to soft sell a masculine image. The main impact of these advertisements was to further Rush's image as a recreational rather than overtly sexual product.

Phase 2:

The next series of advertisements promoted Rush as the drug of the hip, urban gay. In full page, four color advertisements, a giant phallic-shaped bottle of Rush dominates a nocturnal illustration of a Manhattan skyline. The caption reads, "It's the Rush hour/Coast to Coast and Around the World. Have you tried it yet?" Aside from the liquid incense trademark on the bottle (visible in the advertisement), no mention is made as to how the product is used. The advertisment is particularly successful in furthering the notion that Rush is a cosmopolitan activity and an integral, known part of the urban/urbane gay experience.

Pharmex, Ltd. was the first poppers manufacturer to formulate a major, large budget advertising campaign. Phase 2, which is the focal point of the campaign, echoes the disco-styled, gay sensibility that emerged in the late 70's. Rush's high profile image paralleled and in many respects capitalized on the political and social visibility that the gay lifestyle garnered at this time.

The product specially manufactured for Heavy Duty.

Bolt: 1980, <u>Drummer Magazine</u>, © Pacific Western Distributing Corporation

Bolt:

While Rush's "saturday night fever" type advertising proved attractive to a mainstream gay population, it had the potential to disenfranchise the gay consumer attuned to and expectant of explicitly sexual imagery. Bolt, first produced by Pharmex, Ltd. in 1979-80, was aimed specifically at the consumer most often identified with the leather subculture.

Bolt, "The product specifically manufactured for heavy duty," was promoted with well-drawn visuals of macho men engaged in the type of activity common to the erotic literature of the leather subculture. In one typically explicit advertisement (a gas station tableau), a barechested, muscle-bound leather character astride a motorcycle, is shown about to be "gassed up" by an equally masculine pump man. Though the Bolt advertisement, unlike the Rush campaign, projects a sexually literal image, the advertisement (like Rush's) is of particularly high quality, far more sophisticated than those of its competitors.

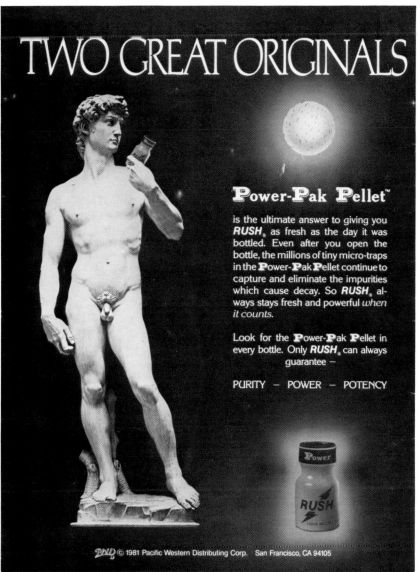

TWO GREAT ORIGINALS

Power-Pak Pellet™

is the ultimate answer to giving you **RUSH** as fresh as the day it was bottled. Even after you open the bottle, the millions of tiny micro-traps in the **Power-Pak Pellet** continue to capture and eliminate the impurities which cause decay. So **RUSH** always stays fresh and powerful *when it counts.*

Look for the **Power-Pak Pellet** in every bottle. Only **RUSH** can always guarantee —

PURITY — POWER — POTENCY

© 1981 Pacific Western Distributing Corp. San Francisco, CA 94105

Phase 3: 1982, Drummer Magazine, © Pacific Western Distributing Corporation

Phase 3:
In the most recent advertisements for Rush, Michelangelo's David clutches the yellow and red vial under the headline "Two Great Originals." The copy in the advertisement stresses the consistency and purity of Rush, with a visual presentation that is lightly satirical yet restrained. Rush is an "original", but in the context of the current controversy on the health hazards of poppers, most interesting is the sense of security the advertisement promotes: Rush is guaranteed and it is pure. The Michelangelo advertisement—sober and visually restrained—capitalizes on the fact that Rush is an established product. The advertisement also reflects a new conservatism apparent in the marketing of some gay-identified products.

Conclusion
The advertising campaign developed by Pharmex, Ltd. for Rush and Bolt are indicative of the consumer extremes to which gay business concerns must appeal. In the entertainment sector, gay enterprises such as bars, bathhouses and magazines find it necessary to design an image which appeals to a specific section of the gay populace. In creating two very distinct promotions—one geared to the emerging mainstream, the other oriented to the leather subculture—Pharmex, Ltd. was able to capture the largest segment of the poppers market.

The promotional strategies created for Rush are in many respects reflective of the changes in political and social consciousness that have taken place in the gay culture. Pharmex, Ltd.'s campaign has proven so effective that the company can claim Rush to be the most popular butyl nitrite produced. According to one company spokesman, the Rush brand has even earned generic identification among a large section of the gay populace.

[1] Fain, Nathan, "How Dangerous Are Poppers?" Stallion, June 1982, p. 69.
[2] Evans, Arthur, "Gay Business vs. Gay Liberation," New York Native, March 1, 1982, p. 10; reprinted from Coming Up!.
[3] The Advocate, June 1978.

"THAT'S IT!"

There's nothing like the feeling you get when you've got the solution.

And nothing else will help you solve problems better, smarter, faster than the Visi™ programs for your personal computer.

For example, our VisiCalc® program: It's #1 in the business because it takes the work out of working with business numbers. The VisiCalc program is the powerful "electronic worksheet" that speeds planning and budgeting. It lets you ask "what if?" and see the answers immediately. So you can analyze the impact of decisions before you make them.

Our VisiTrend/Plot™ program combines graphics with forecasting and statistics. It automatically performs complex calculations and produces charts and graphs. So you can analyze the past, forecast the future and plot your results in an easy-to-understand visual form.

© 1982 VisiCorp

In addition, our series includes the VisiFile™, VisiDex™, VisiSchedule™, VisiPlot™, VisiTerm™ and Desktop/PLAN™ programs.

But the Visi programs are far more than individual problem-solvers. They're all inter-related, just like your needs and tasks, to give you a fully integrated solution.

All of the Visi programs work in much the same way, and they automatically interchange data, too. So it's easy to learn and use any of them, work in many different ways with all of them.

They're brought to you by VisiCorp™. The one company whose only business is helping you make the most of the personal computer in your business.

Ask your retail computer

store salesperson for a demonstration of the Visi series. They'll help you and your computer do all the things you're intent on doing.

THE VISISERIES FROM
VISICORP™
PERSONAL SOFTWARE™

"THAT'S IT!"

To DHL the world is one big desk.

1 CUAL ES LA INTENCION DE LA FOTOGRAFIA,
2 CUAL ES LA INTENCION DEL TEXTO.

Your Daily Newspaper

Your Daily International Newspaper

The newspaper on the left you know, the one on the right you might not. The Financial Times is the primary source of business information for European and, increasingly, U.S. and other world business leaders.

In fact, to ensure you do receive a complete picture of the international business world we have 255 specialist journalists and 18 foreign bureaus around the world. That's three times as many foreign bureaus as the paper on the left.

Never before has international competition been so fierce nor the need for American executives to get a fast and deep view of the international business world been so great.

That's why the international edition, printed in Frankfurt, leaves for New York ahead of the sun on a 4 a.m. flight, connects with our delivery system and is then rushed to you.

Financial Times

Europe's business newspaper
now for the International American.

GIVEN TWO IDENTICAL PHOTOGRAPHS WITH TWO DIFFERENT TEXTS:

Your Daily Newspaper

Your Daily International Newspaper

THE WORLD'S MOST ADVANCED COPIER LOOKS EVEN BETTER THIS YEAR.

1 WHAT IS THE INTENTION OF THE PHOTOGRAPH,
2 WHAT IS THE INTENTION OF THE TEXT.

Anyway You Look At It ... ADM Has Your Antenna !

From 1980 - 1981, I collected over 1,000 pieces of technical information. The information was vendor literature, reports, charts, graphs, requests for proposals, etc. The information was collected by contacting scientific equipment vendors, visiting companies in Silicon Valley, going to trade shows, visiting technical libraries, and reading technical journals. To help get this information, I started my own company - OK RESEARCH. In March 1981, I used about 500 pieces of the information in an installation at SITE in San Francisco. The installation examined the relationships between art and technology using the technical information as source documents.

The vendor literature used in this article was selected from this information base.

Salesmen at NEPCON 80   -   San Mateo, California, 1980

As "our" art merges with philosophy and literature, approaches technology tentatively, becomes information (this publication for instance), "their" technology usurps our place as maker of things, imitator of nature, courtier to those in power, interpretor of the unknown.

The shifting roles of technology, art, and religion are reflected with hard sell distortion in the vendor "literature" produced by those who sell the products of technology. In an ad for "high technology products that contribute to our country's defense posture", United Technologies says "Technology is a continuing response to the needs of life." (Military Science and Technology 1 (1):21, 1981) According to a Gilson Medical Electronics ad "Liquid chromatography is an art." (American Laboratory 12(8):16, 1980) Datacopy says their series 200 Factory Data Entry System is "the ultimate solution." (Datacopy brochure, 1980)

"Standing in the Illinois prairie, the Fermi Lab accelerator was one of the engineering wonders of the world, a veritable cathedral of science." Calder, Nigel, THE KEY TO THE UNIVERSE, Middlesex, England, Penguin, 1978. p. 10

"No poem, no play, no piece of music written since then comes near the theory of relativity in its power as one strains to apprehend it, to make the mind tremble with delight." Judson, Horace Freeland, The Rage To Know, ATLANTIC 245(4):116, 1980

"The right answers again & again"
Brochure for Bausch & Lomb spectronic® 2000 spectrophotometer, 1980

OK research

2000 Center Street #1340 Berkeley CA 94704

23 November 1980

ADM
P.O. Box 1178
Poplar Bluff
MP 63901

Gentlemen:

I am collecting and displaying technical information. I would appreciate receiving any brochures/information you have available on your 11 foot polar mount antenna.

Thank you for your attention.

Sincerely,

Judy Malloy

Judy Malloy,
President

Although vendor literature isn't the real literature of technology, it may be of more cultural interest. The literature of technology is journal articles, reports, proceedings, etc. which must pass review boards and conform to rigid style guides. The writers, scientists and engineers, are not always capable of clarity, nor is clarity always in the economic interest of their sponsoring intitutions. Technical papers are difficult to read, even for their audience, and they allow little of the philosophy and values of the technical community to leach.

Vendor literature, however, is generally not produced by those who created the product. It's made by salesmen and managers. Some of it has strong information value - hard facts about hardware that are hard to find in journal articles, and specifications, that if archived may be of use to a testing engineer investigating a failure 10 years later. All of it, however, is ADVERTISING.

In full page layouts in the pages of American Laboratory, Chemical Week, Aviation Week and Space Technology, Genetic Engineering News, or, in neat stacks in salesmen's silver briefcases, technical advertising preaches salvation through technology.

"THE AMAZING PIEZOTRON" (Kistler Advanced Dynamic Instrumentation brochure, n.d.)

"WE HAVE THE VISION TO PUT VHSIC TO WORK" (Westinghouse ad, Military Science and Technology 1(1):14, 1981)

"BIRTH OF A LEGEND....NATIONAL MICROTECH INC. INTRODUCES THE APOLLO X9 SATELLITE ANTENNA" (Satellite Communications 5(10):2, 1981)

"UNLOCK HIDDEN SECRETS WITH HUGHES COLOR TELEVISION THERMOGRAPHY" (Industrial Research and Development 23(12):77, 1981)

"WE'VE GOT A DIRECT POWERLINE TO THE SUN FOR YOU" (Solarex ad, IEEE Spectrum 18(11):1981)

"WE'RE EXPANDING THE WORLD'S VIEW" (Ad for Fusion, Military Science and Technology 1(1):53, 1981)

"ANYWAY YOU LOOK AT IT...ADM HAS YOUR ANTENNA" (ADM brochure, 1980)

It is disturbing that at a time when family structure is unpredictable and creationism unbelievable, Bausch & Lomb may have "the right answers again & again." We can question whether Listerine cures the common cold, but Italtd. probably does "know how to channel time." (Telecommunications Journal 48(1): 18, 1981)

"And you'll do it all in _real_ real Time..."
ad for Advanced Micro Devices RTE 8/8800 real-time emulator Electronics 53(17):11, 1980

Those who advertise the products of technology promise not only solutions and salvation, but also, like most other advertisers, they imply that the use of their products will ensure wealth, distinction, individuality, and success.

"BREAK OUT OF YOUR MOLD"   (Norchem ad for molding resins, Modern Plastics 56(8):68, 1979)

"FOR ADVENTURE I WORK AT RAYCHEM"   (Chemical and Engineering News 58(43):14, 1980)

"EVERYTHING LOOKS RICHER IN ULTRAMARINE"   (Whittaker, Clark and Daniels, inc. ad, Modern Plastics 56(11):9, 1979)

"THIS IS YOU INVITATION TO SUBSCRIBE TO A FRANKLY ELITIST MAGAZINE"   (letter advertising Military Science and Technology, received 1981)

"Make your mark on the world"
Quantrad brochure, 1980

A Quantrad brochure advertising laser scribers says, "Make your mark on the world." It's illustrated by a stunning photo of oranges. The word "Quantrad" is imprinted on one of the oranges.

A Kay-Fries Chemicals ad shows a "perfectly" photographed stretch of sand with 3 small bird tracks - "IF: if you utilize silane coupling agents to bond inorganic materials with organic polymers, these three steps can put you on the right track." (Modern Plastics 55(10):21, 1978)

A Perkin-Elmer ad shows a splendid sunset: "IMAGINE.... an automated, multielement AA system that will determine 6 elements in 50 samples at record speed. (American Laboratory 10(2):35, 1978)

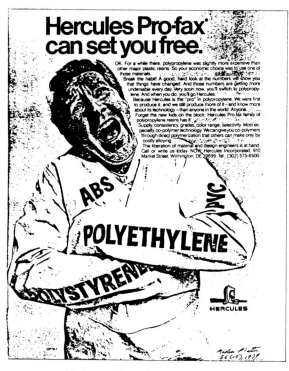

Modern Plastics 56(10), 1979
Xerox copy, J. Malloy

These ads are compelling, "beautiful".   They may not stir imaginations, but they say they do. They catch the eye. An orange is more reassuring than a laser scriber. A sunset is more "natural" than an automated, multielement AA system. Like artists, engineers and scientists want to make their mark on the world. And, while "we" are integrating technology into our performances, installations, and publications, "they" would like to be considered artists. It is likely that our idea of technology is as flawed in their eyes as their idea of art is in ours.

"CREATING BRILLIANT LAKE COLORS IS AN ART"   (Modern Plastics 54(1):69, 1977)

"PICTURE YOUR DATA THE WAY YOU WANT IT" (Hewlett Packard ad for a graphics work station using the HP 2647A intelligent terminal, Chemical Week 129(14), 1981)

"EVERY PICTURE TELLS A STORY....AND ALL OUR STORIES HAVE HAPPY ENDINGS" (ad for Gallenkamp incubators, Nature 293(5830), 1981

"Liquid chromatography is an art"
Gilson ad, American Laboratory   12(9):16, 1980

These two ads appeared in a 1965 issue of Scientific American:

Universal Oil Products ad for BHA, Scientific
American 213(5), 1965   *xerox copy, J.Malloy*

Xerox ad, Scientific American 213(5),
1965   *xerox copy, J.Malloy*

Today it's:

"BIO LOGICALS BRINGS YOU SAME DAY DNA"   (Nature 294(5842):back cover, 1981)

"A NEW, FASTER WAY TO CLONE OR SEQUENCE"   (P. L Biochemicals, inc., Science
                                    214 (4519):389, 1981)
"YES, ♪♫ WE HAVE MONOCLONALS ♫♪ WE HAVE MONOCLONALS TODAY! ♪ "   (Accurate Chemical
                                and Scientific Corp. ad, Nature 295(5847), 1982)
"START CLEAN....SWEEP CLEAN....STAY CLEAN"   (Stauffer Chemicals ad for Eptam®
                                herbicide, Sun-Diamond Grower 2(1):14, 1981)
"OUR NEW TEST TUBE BABY"   (MSE Scientific Instruments ad for MSE Micro-Centaur
                        centrifuge, Nature 295(5851), 1982)

"Send in the clones... we have the buffers"

Research Organics inc ad , Genetic Engineering News
1(4):14, 1981

Space Invaders or The Failure of the Present

The legendary desire of the '60's created a legacy of private spectacle almost before it was over: the rock opera "Tommy" performed by the Who "where a deaf, dumb and blind kid sure plays a mean pin-ball." He lives in a private world untouched by the social acts of school or the stifling normalcy of the family. Instead, his mother becomes an acid queen, his step-father turns into Fagan; he is the new orphan boy, Oliver Twist who as we remember, can't be missed. His only contact with the outside world, his way of being "in touch" is through the mystical experience he has with his pin-ball machine. Even though throughout the opera he is crying, "See me, Feel me, Touch me, Heal me. . . ." But this is always directed to the mass audience he can not see, but assumes is watching, and not to any of the individuals who make up his world. Shaped by acid, a self-induced spiritualism, he is trying desperately to regress; for in the movie he is an adult who is also refusing childhood, an adult who has no refuse, an adult who lives in a private self-contained world of spectacle: the world of acid with its desires for inner peace and non-contamination, where inner and outer space appear to match, where daily life is transformed into a glorious spectacle filled with the imaginary truth of the cosmos. Is this what really happened to the NASA space program? After they went to the moon, we dropped acid, to celebrate.

The notion of private spectacle cuts through contemporary notions of the history of the imagination or to put it another way as Wilhelm Reich asked, "How could the masses be made to desire their own repression?" What could further alienate one person from another more than possibility or private spectacle engaging the participant so completely, and including all his senses so that she/he feels transformed — into another state, taken to another plane, the Zen-like threshold of mediation; the release into the cosmos of the unfettered subject who no longer has a care about the world. He has truly escaped and yet he is not mad, nor even a schizophrenic, but how did it happen, and what happens when he returns as he inevitably must?

It is no longer the star child born of "2001" who is able to glue together the desire for a new fantasy: rebirth achieved beyond the marvel of technology — somewhere else, where everything is different. But "Alien," the monster who eats your insides, who sucks the face, the eyes, but who does not kill, whose desire is unknown, unknowable and who is lurking everywhere, who is uncontainable, who fills every opening, every orifice, and who even when expunged remains still there somehow and even more unknown — omnipresent; saying more about lack/loss of memory, fear/failure of the present than the fear of the unknown, for haven't there always been monsters in the movies caught in the airlock infecting the very air we breathe? What is it that is omnipresent?

"Tommy: a rock opera", Ken Russell, 1977

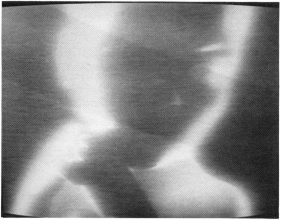

"2001, A Space Odyssey", Stanley Kubrick, 1968

"Alien", 1979

Video Arcade, Chicago, 1982

Once upon a time before writing there were other systems for memory, other methodologies for inserting the spectator who would be a player into the fabric, the design of life, the design of remembrances. Giulio Camillo's memory theatre for one, which reversed the relationship of participant to theatre where for one hour by occupying the center of the stage the spectator who would play could master the universe by letting his mind crystallize around the mystical array of knowledge amassed here, an amassing that included the Cabala as well as what would become science and the cogito. Magic assumes laws and forces running through the universe which the operator can use once she/he knows how to capture them. This system of memory was known as a memory theatre, attached to a building, an actual theatre, but where the spectator/player occupied the center stage and where the audience was replaced by these shelves of knowledge which were held in a diachronic as well as a synchronic relation, allowing the spectator/player the advantage of traveling in time, a system for memorizing the past to be used in controlling the future: except of course that that concept did not yet exist. This was perhaps the first terminal (as implied by the neutral and power-effacing terminology of computer-talk). A terminal as a final place of being as one looked, one did not see, because one was imagining, actually imaging the objects, the referents to which were tied an involutable and inseparable knowledge, a knowledge which included the certainty that this was the way in which man could be in control and one which by the way refused the domain of reason although it was certainly leading up to it.

This was the time before the Enlightenment, before reason had encircled anything in its path, before the great history lessons had carved up the city into parcels of cynicism and displaced all feeling, before discourses and psychoanalysis, before our time, we can only imagine ourselves; this was a private theatre in which to make the human whole, where she/he could become: it was even more private, available to only one for sure, its creator, beyond democracy and even guilt.

The inscription of the look in the realm of the imaginary defined the resurgence of the theatre in the renaissance. The private look of the king was unveiled in a public forum, where the demands for, the desire for a unified mass could be expressed and a collective fantasy shared. This look was set in place through perspective, a proven method for setting the world in order as well as a way of naturalizing spectacle, allowing it to become ritualized, a recognized part of everyday life. This was a private theatre for the king where even his subjects were on display, where all who were loyal and bore allegiance came to express their devotion. And yet, he was on display as well, expressing his dominion. This private theatre of the king shaped the subjects, constructed the masses in his own image, before

Arby's Restaurant, Penn Station, N.Y.C., 1982

The Memory Theatre of Giulo Camillo
based on l'Idea del Theatro

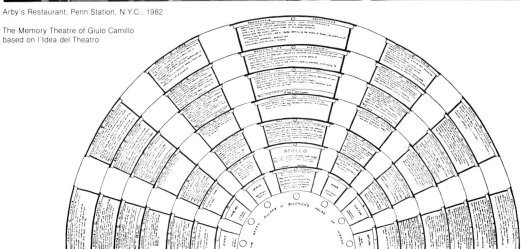

top
Hugo Ball,
1916

bottom
Pablo Picasso,
1910

discourses led to the fragmentation and the variety of looks that such a fragmented subject would assume; and ultimately a private theatre, a discourse of an alienated self, too absorbed in games of mastery and control (chance) to notice.

The television is the screen of alienation, located in the home. Its mirror is opaque, we are fractured and deformed by reflection. This television set which blots out the family even as it spectacularizes the home calls attention to the family unit in opposition to the city. It isn't "big brother" who watches, it is we who watch for "it," in a reverse of surveillance, looking for signs that something is there, hoping that the endless repetitions which pass over our eyes will reveal what we hope is hidden, that which will make us feel whole and connected, that which will provide a reconciliation. But the city can not come into the living room, it is repressed through representation like a dream image whose overt content suppresses that which is latent. In the order of the news what is omnipresent is only chaos and disintegration, what is represented can not be believed. From the vantage point of the living room, she/he feels their attack, the masses that crowd the speaker in front of the stage. She/he knows she/he is different, she/he must escape. The look of the king could be appropriated and made one's own. And in a private theatre who is left to care? Video games go the television set, characterized by the viewer being connected to the rest of the world in so far as she/he is separated in the living room, one better; for no longer does he even see the world, now she/he is connected only to a secret fantasy brought out in cartoon fashion by the animated sequences that deny the "impression of reality," that deny the city and daily life and will not allow for its return.

With video games we play knowing that we will lose. Our strategy is to react, to fire first, to try to discern the all important rules for discourse that determine the length of time before we will be shot out of the sky, before we must try to return. There is no overt narrative to link us to the past, no shared fantasy with the others around us, no longing or memory. Only the present and a barrage of lights and action and the over-powering feeling that we are really there or here somehow more alive than before.

The body in space, floating, replaces the essentiality of drama, but was this always the case? Hugo Ball transformed himself into a marionette, a mannequin celebrating the reduction of man to a machine. Celebrating or lamenting, it is unclear. The Italian Futurists saw the metropolitan universe as devoid of sense or place, expressing a nostalgia for the future as well as the past. As George Simmel remarked, "Pure nervous stimulation was the foundation of metro-politan activity." The din of the city is seen as the sole reality; the joke, the agonized attitude converge in a re-iterated suicide attempt to teach those who can understand to laugh at moral and material pain. By 1922 the mannequin jester was transformed into a clown capable of assuming a new identity, of pleasing those he serves, of prodding the Unconscious into a positivistic reconcilation of humankind with the city as a living machine; and we are all equal and all the same we machines. From then on writes Manfred Tafuri, the constructivist theatre sets its self up as the model for a positive relation between man and machine, not because the cause of alienation has vanished, but rather because it has become greater. The Russian constructivist Mejerchol'd's method became that of wrapping within work the need for play, where this play could be taken back to the beehive of production and enslaved by it. Within a maximum of planning and mechanization (and therefore only by total alienation) could mass humankind re-explode into a collective laborfesta, liberated by the sacrificial rites of Dadaism, the disbelief in it all — the body trapped by its machines has no hope of being free. It shows up its own imperfections with the Soviet experiences of the early 1920's: it is no longer the theatre which went into the city, but the city that re-entered the theatre, the bio-mechanical acrobat had become the prophet of a society of total work. Oscar Schlemmer's marionette who lived by the creed: all that can be mechanized must be mechanized, result — we can see that which can not be mechanized. A big yes that reduces humankind to being a marionette liberates the same marionette, for the mannequin is 'that body which either has no consciousness at all or an infinite one; that is to say either a marionette or a god.''

Catalogue essay reprinted from International Cultural Center Antwerp, Belgium, June 1982

Oscar Schlemmer:
Dance of too Sticks, 1929

Fortunato Depero,
Mani onetta balli plastici, 1916

Lyubov Popova:
stage construction for le loco
magnifiguo by Crommelynck,
production Mejerchol'd, 1922

82   Judith Barry

SELLING THE FUTURE

Prediction is very difficult, especially about the future.
— Niels Bohr

By the year 2000

OUR FUTURE

YOUR FUTURE

WHY LEAP INTO THE FUTURE WHEN YOU CAN WADE INTO IT?

INTO THE FUTURE

Building the future ...for you.

the future

AMRAAM... for command of the skies of tomorrow.

for tomorrow

L'avenir:
nous occupons la ligne

JEUMONT-SCHNEIDER
Concrétise l'avenir de la téléphonie.

L'avenir

THE FUTURE

for tomorrow

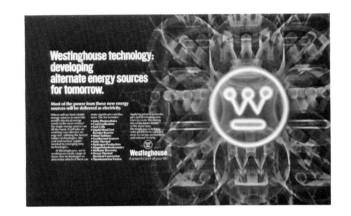

the future

By the year 2000

OUR FUTURE

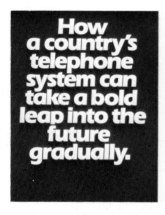

into the future

their future

INTO THE 21st CENTURY

Invading the information age.

American Telephone and Telegraph
(AT&T, Western Electric, Bell System, Long Lines, Bell Labs)

"AT&T now exercises control of varying degree over every form of American communications transmission — from the telephone instrument in your home or office to the press association dispatches in your newspaper and the network television programs in your living room; veritably, the nerve system of our society."

Monopoly[1]

Who will lead the communications software invasion?

Within a decade of the invention of the telephone in 1876, the foundations had been laid for the "Biggest Company on Earth"[2] through a combination of monopolistic business practice and the public relations savvy of two-time Bell president, Theodore Vail. Creating a public image of the company as a "natural monopoly," Vail proceeded to annex Western Electric (the largest manufacturer of electrical equipment in the U.S.), and completed the incorporation of the conglomerate as American Telephone and Telegraph. He launched his second term of office (1907-19) by fabricating the "One System, One Policy, Universal Service" ad campaign to gain favorable public opinion while AT&T bought up or drove out the remaining vestiges of a competitive telephone market. By 1909 Bell had also gained control of Western Union's telegraph service. With threats of anti-trust action, Vail initiated a "Regulation: It's Wonderful" theme for the 1913 Annual Report. Unimpressed by the tactic, Congress did act and divestiture was completed later that year resulting in AT&T's withdrawal from its brief venture into the telegraph business.

Within this context, the anti-trust settlement of 1982 between AT&T and the Department of Justice may have a familiar ring.
"In recent months, it has become increasingly clear to outsiders and AT&T officials alike that the government's case against Bell — particularly its documentation of 'predatory' policies designed to exclude potential competitors from long distance markets — was very strong."[3]
Newsweek, Jan. 18, 1982

The settlement forced AT&T to divest itself of its 22 local companies, representing two thirds of its assets. In return, divestiture now makes it possible for AT&T *to program* as well as transmit information in an attempt to gain control of the new high technology telecommunications markets in computerized data processing, cable-TV, and electronic mail.

The recent action makes it perfectly clear that Bell no longer wants to be merely your telephone company:
"The end result [of the consent decree] in any case will be a new relationship between the phone user and the organization he or she came to know as the 'telephone company.'"[4]
Charles L. Brown, Chairman AT&T.

But the advertisements have been telling us that all along.

WE will. We're Western Electric. And some of the most important products we make for the Bell System are the computer programs known as software. Software is the step-by-step instructions that tell the hardware of your communications system how to function; what to do.

While past advertising campaigns have served primarily promotional and public relations functions, AT&T's new advertising strategies have emerged in response to continuing legal problems and as a result of competition in existing and potential markets.[5]

(After all, it's just not enough to 'Reach Out and Touch Someone' any longer, MCI, Sprint, and Western Union have begun to chip away at some of that lucrative long distance market enabling people to 'reach out' and 'touch' for less.)

Restructuring the Bell System will open a whole new world of communications.

There is no cause and effect relation between the proposed consent decree and the price of phone service.

This ad appeared in the January 17, 1982 issue of the *Chapel Hill Newspaper*:

"*The restructuring we agreed to will, as you know, separate the local companies from AT&T. In this new arrangement your telephone promises to give you greater access to the benefits of the Information Age.*"

The appeal to the local customer is the claim that "*There is no cause and effect relation between the proposed consent decree and the price of phone service.*"

On January 28th (eleven days later) the same paper carried the news of Southern Bell's proposed rate increases that amounted to approximately 40% for monthly services and to over 300% for connection charges.

In an effort to formulate this country's telecommunications policy, the Congress has been working for years (against extreme pressures from special interest groups, especially AT&T) to update the now antiquated Communications Act of 1934, under which the FCC is still operating.

The advertisement (excerpted below, appeared in the *New York Times*, June 20, 1982) was directed at stockholders rather than customers, and included a headline in the body of the text that read: "*Please speak out for your country and your company.*" This was part of AT&T's successful campaign to block the proposed legislation.

An urgent message to AT&T share owners:
The anti-Bell bill continues to move through Congress. The time to speak out is now.

If H.R. 5158 becomes law, it will aid foreign competition, handcuff Bell Laboratories' research, and force Bell customers to subsidize other companies for years to come.

The proposed Telecommunications Act of 1982 (HR 5158) deals not only with issues directly related to AT&T but to:

". . . insure the First Amendment goal of public access to the fullest diversity of information sources. In writing HR 5158, we were concerned that allowing Bell to transmit information it owned or controlled over its own monopoly long-distance facilities would create 'bottlenecks' to access information, reducing diversity."[6]

Rep. Timothy E. Wirth, chairman of the House Subcommittee on Telecommunications, Consumer Protection and Finance.

The knowledge business

The familiar AT&T logo of the bell enclosed in a circle is now accompanied by the words: ***"The knowledge business."***

"From the beginning, knowledge has shaped the future. Now America is entering a new age, the information age."

AT&T's promotional techniques of appropriating terminology such as 'knowledge business' and 'information age' is dealt with by Enzensberger's concept of the 'consciousness industry':

"The mind industry can take on anything, digest it, reproduce it, and pour it out." ". . . it is capable of transforming any idea into a slogan, any work of the imagination into a hit."[7]

The telephone has not only become an essential and integral part of daily life, it can serve, in some respects, as a model two-way telecommunication system in which the individual can determine the purpose, time frame, and content of the message transmitted.

While the actual abuses of the telephone are well known, (by AT&T and the government in the form of illegal wiretapping and eavesdropping), the new technologies create an even greater threat in matters pertaining to invasion of privacy and widespread surveillance.

But a problem may also lie in the new emphasis on the telephone as a *receiver* of commercially programmed information where the message *content* as well as the *medium* of transmission is centrally controlled. In these terms, the pervasive qualities of this media network presents an immediate similarity to television:

"TV, by virtue of its mere presence, is a social control in itself. There is no need to imagine it as a state periscope spying on everyone's private life — the situation as it stands is more efficient than that: *it is the certainty the people are no longer speaking to each other*, that they are definitely isolated in the face of a speech without response."[8]

This kind of 'speech without response' mechanism within a telephone system could undoubtedly have devastating cultural effects, especially when you consider that most of the new, so-called 'interactive' media (e.g.: video games and QUBE's cable-TV) work in similar ways to create the illusion of 'two-way' response — limiting dialogue between people rather than promoting conversation and discourse.[9]

Although AT&T may have given up more than was initially anticipated with the consent decree, control of 'the world's most sophisticated computer network' in the hands of one, or relatively few suppliers is the ultimate prize. And if this is the case, the *'Knowledge Business'* could be perceived as AT&T's latest attempt to make the world safe for *'monopoly'* again.

"Will the telephone customer be better off in the future?

[1]Goulden, Joseph C. *Monopoly*, 1968.
[2]from Kleinfield, Sonny *The Biggest Company on Earth, A Profile of AT&T*, 1981.
[3]Pauly, David et al "Ma Bell's Big Breakup" *Newsweek*, Jan. 18, 1982.
[4]Brown, Charles L. "Bell A Vindication Of Our Stand" *New York Times*, Aug. 15, 1982.
[5]Two major court decisions caused changes in the AT&T monopoly during the 1970's: "Carterfone", was responsible for permitting the use of other manufacturers' telephones and auxiliary equipment; and "MCI", along with other independent companies, won permission to compete in the long-distance market.
[6]Wirth, Timothy, "The AT&T Settlement:. . . ." *New York Times*, Aug. 15, 1982.
[7]Enzenberger, Hans Magnus *The Consciousness Industry*, 1974.
[8]Baudrillard, Jean *For A Critique of the Political Economy of the Sign*, 1981.
[9]D'Agostino, Peter "Proposal for QUBE" *Teleguide*, 1980.

advertising

art

ad·ver·tis·ing *n* **1 :** the action of calling something to the attention of the public esp. by paid announcements **2 :** ADVERTISEMENTS **3 :** the business of preparing advertisements for publication or broadcast

In an advertisement, we are told that we *do* choose, we *are* free individuals, we have taste, style, uniqueness, and we *will act accordingly.* In other words, having been attributed with the qualities connected with a product, we are projected as buyers of it, precisely because 'given' that we 'have' the beliefs implied in the ad, we will act in accordance with them and buy the product that embodies those beliefs. It is a sort of double-bind.—Judith Williamson

Advertising has occupied a peculiar corner of American culture for a long time, because it is the subject of widely ambivalent emotional and cognitive dispositions. On the one hand, it is seen as a necessary lubricant of commerce. On the other, it is construed as annoying legerdemain, economic waste and cultural dross. Both points of view have meaning in contemporary life, and evidence exists that both are true—up to a point.—George N. Gordon

Advertising, so overwhelmingly dominated by the US, is an important historical factor of the West's version of a free press.—Anthony Smith

The historians and archaeologists will one day discover that the ads of our time are the richest and most faithful daily reflections that any society ever made of its entire range of activities.—Marshall McLuhan

Publicity has in fact understood the tradition of the oil painting more thoroughly than most art historians. —John Berger

art \'ärt\ *n* [ME, fr. OF, fr. L *art-, ars* — more at ARM] **1 a :** skill in performance acquired by experience, study, or observation **: KNACK b :** human ingenuity in adapting natural things to man's use **2 a :** a branch of learning: (1) : one of the humanities (2) *pl* **:** the liberal arts **b** *archaic* **:** LEARNING, SCHOLARSHIP **3 a :** an occupation requiring knowledge or skill **: TRADE b :** a system of rules or methods of performing particular actions **c :** systematic application of knowledge or skill in effecting a desired result **4 a :** the conscious use of skill, taste, and creative imagination in the production of aesthetic objects; *also* **:** works so produced **b :** the craft of the artist **c** (1) **:** FINE ARTS (2) **:** one of the fine arts (3) **:** a graphic art **5 a** *archaic* **:** a skilful plan **b :** ARTFULNESS

. . . art lies half-way between scientific knowledge and mythical or magical thought. It is common knowledge that the artist is both something of a scientist and of a 'bricoleur'. By his craftsmanship he constructs a material object which is also an object of knowledge. —Claude Levi-Strauss

Our fine arts were developed, their types and uses were established, in times very different from the present, by men whose power of action upon things was insignificant in comparison with ours. But the amazing growth of our techniques, the adaptability and precision they have attained, the ideas and habits they are creating, make it a certainty that profound changes are impending in the ancient craft of the Beautiful. —Paul Valery

By its nature, art is *organic*, which means that it is free neither of material nor mechanistic constraints but that it has the desire to transcend these limitations. Whether art's constraining forces are American businessmen or Russian commissars, ultimately they succeed only in suppressing the cathartic and liberating value of art as a vehicle for social evolution. —Hans Haacke

Compared with the often one-dimensional optimisim of propaganda, art is permeated with pessimism, not seldom intertwined with comedy. Its "liberating laughter" recalls the danger and the evil that have passed—this time! But the pessimism of art is not counterrevolutionary. It serves to warn against the "happy consciousness" of radical praxis: as if all of that which art invokes and indicts could be settled through the class struggle.—Herbert Marcuse

Scientifically treated, art stands on the same ground as religion and philosophy.—Hegel

Though one part of the modern movement in art, the expressionist and surrealist wing, has taken refuge in unconditioned fantasies almost unconnected with any outer perceptions or activities, another part, that begun by the cubists and constructivists, has sought to find equivalent symbols for the activities of science and the forms of the machine.—Lewis Mumford

Art is not the reflection of reality, it is the reality of that reflection.—Jean-Luc Godard

communication

corporation

com·mu·ni·ca·tion \kə-ˌmyü-nə-ˈkā-shən\ n **1** : an act or instance of transmitting **2 a** : information communicated **b** : a verbal or written message **3 a** : an exchange of information **4** pl **a** : a system (as of telephones) for communicating **b** : a system of routes for moving troops, supplies, and vehicles **c** : personnel engaged in communicating **5** : a process by which meanings are exchanged between individuals through a common system of symbols **6** pl but sing or pl in constr **a** : a technique for expressing ideas effectively in speech or writing or through the arts **b** : the technology of the transmission of information

cor·po·ra·tion \ˌkȯr-pə-ˈrā-shən\ n **1 a** obs : a group of merchants or traders united in a trade guild **b** : the municipal authorities of a town or city **2** : a body formed and authorized by law to act as a single person although constituted by one or more persons and legally endowed with various rights and duties including the capacity of succession **3** : an association of employers and employees in a basic industry or of members of a profession organized as an organ of political representation in a corporative state **4** : POTBELLY

The term "communication" comes from the Latin *communis* (common) or *communicare* (to establish a community or a commonness, or to share). At least it is clear that the term implies a sharing, a meeting of minds, a bringing about of a common set of symbols in the minds of the participants—in short, an understanding . . . It should be reiterated here that we are considering communication as a *process*, not as a synonym for "message."—John C. Merril/Ralph R. Lowenstein

The means of liberation of a class are determined by empiric relations; and among them, the conditions of the means of communication.—Marx and Engels

As the mass media of communication in North America serve primarily as a platform for advertisers, the personal motives of communicators and their mass media are invariably subordinated to economic motives. The name of the game is *sell* or *communicate* (these verbs are used synonymously in media jargon) and derive a profit. All media are corporate enterprises in the United States. Corporate enterprises exist primarily as economic profit-making entities. Profit is what media is all about.—Wilson Bryan Key

When a medium of communication has the power to disembody words, to split them away from their original source, the psychological and social effects of language are forever changed. In such an environment, language becomes something more than a mode of communication. It becomes an object of contemplation.
—Neil Postman

And 'context' is linked to another undefined notion called 'meaning.' Without context, words and actions have no meaning at all. This is true not only of human communication in words but also of all communication whatsoever, of all mental process, of all mind, including that which tells the sea anemone how to grow and the amoeba what he should do next.
—Gregory Bateson

As for the radio's object, I don't think it can consist merely in prettifying public life. Nor is radio in my view an adequate means of bringing back coziness to the home and making family life bearable again. But quite apart from the dubiousness of its functions, radio is one-sided when it should be two-. It is purely an apparatus for distribution, for mere sharing out. So here is a positive suggestion: change this apparatus over from distribution to communication. The radio would be the finest possible communication apparatus in public life, a vast network of pipes.—Bertolt Brecht

It is generally believed that modern communications systems must inevitably destroy all local cultures. This is because these systems have largely been used for the benefit of the center and not as two-way streets. Today, unchecked mass communication bullies and shouts humanity into silence and passivity.
—Alan Lomax

Feudalism was an emotional system of corporate loyalties tied to a shared image, like a primitive totem symbol. Feudalism melted before the impact of gunpowder and printing. Such is the modern corporation.
—Marshall McLuhan

Modern technology—the people as well as the things—became a vehicle of corporate power, an extension of authority, a reinforcement of existing social relations. No wonder, then, that modern technology has lost its magic and predictions of liberation through science ring so hollow.—David Noble

The public relations policy of a company is of key importance in evaluating its character. What a corporation does in this area provides an index to the true objectives of the organization, to the operational codes of the policy makers, and to their general conception of the role their company plays in the total social structure. For the public relations function is essentially the specialized use of communication as an *ideological* instrument of corporate policy.
—Richard Ellis

. . . regardless of whether they belong to the military-industrial complex, are composed of profit-seeking individuals or groups. Corporations have a tendency to place their welfare above that of people or environment. One artist or a group of artist-planners for each corporation in proportion to its size might mellow the negative impact that many corporations have on social organisms. I am not merely calling for the emergence of the artist-conservationist; ideally, I mean that the artist, along with conscientious scientists, should turn Elizabeth, N.J. into a less suffocating environment.
—Otto Piene

In a technocratic society—so I suggested—political authority is based upon a mystique of scientific expertise. That is what supposedly guarantees the competence of the state and private corporations to keep an intricate industrial economy functioning. If people are to acquiesce in that mystique, they must pledge their deep psychic allegiance to the world view of modern science and the industrial disciplines that support the myth of progress.—Theodore Roszak

culture

ideology

cul·ture \'kəl-chər\ n [ME, fr. MF, fr. L *cultura*, fr. *cultus*, pp.] **1** : CULTIVATION, TILLAGE **2** : the act of developing the intellectual and moral faculties esp. by education **3** : expert care and training ⟨beauty ~⟩ **4** : enlightenment and excellence of taste acquired by intellectual and aesthetic training **5 a** : a particular stage of advancement in civilization **b** : the characteristic features of such a stage or state **c** : behavior typical of a group or class **6** : cultivation of living material in prepared nutrient media; *also* : a product of such cultivation

One of the functions of culture is to provide a highly selective screen between man and the outside world. In its many forms, culture therefore designates what we pay attention to and what we ignore.
—Edward T. Hall

If we understand by culture what it originally meant (the Roman *cultura*—derived from *colere*, to take care of and preserve and cultivate) then we can say without any exaggeration that a society obsessed with consumption cannot at the same time be cultured or produce a culture.—Hannah Arendt

. . . the development of mass culture (bourgeois culture) is rooted in the technology of mass communication—sophisticated electronic instruments such as radio and television. These devices force the situation whereby the cultural media are used for large-scale manipulation and effective political control. *But we can turn them off!*—Joseph Berke

By surrounding the consumer with images of the good life, and by associating them with the glamour of celebrity and success, mass culture encourages the ordinary man to cultivate extraordinary tastes, to identify himself with the privileged minority against the rest, and to join them, in his fantasies, in a life of exquisite comfort and sensual refinement.
—Christopher Lasch

For Levi-Strauss, there is an underlying structure to culture, which is the laws of thought, the properties of mind which are everywhere the same. Thus, *au fond*, there is a Ur-form, a synchronic "mytheme" which, like a monad, holds all culture in its single embrace. For structuralism, culture is the hidden code of significant form. For me, culture is the set of answers, coherent or discordant, the anguished responses to the significant questions of human existence.—Daniel Bell

The very term Popular culture has unconsciously become a wall protecting serious art from the competition of the more sophisticated and gifted creatures, the platinum huns, as it were, in the . . . world out there . . .—Tom Wolfe

The bastard form of mass culture is humiliated repetition: content, ideological schema, the blurring of contradictions—these are repeated, but the superficial forms are varied: always new books, new programs, new films, news items, but always the same meaning.
—Roland Barthes

ide·ol·o·gy \-'äl-ə-jē\ *also* ide·al·o·gy \-'äl-ə-jē, -'al-\ n [F *idéologie*, fr. *idéo*- ideo- + -*logie* -logy] **1** : visionary theorizing **2 a** : a systematic body of concepts esp. about human life or culture **b** : a manner or the content of thinking characteristic of an individual, group, or culture **c** : the integrated assertions, theories, and aims that constitute a sociopolitical program

If in all ideology men and their circumstances appear upside-down as in a *camera obscura*, this phenomenon arises just as much from their historical life-process as the inversion of objects on the retina does from their physical life-process.—Karl Marx

The response to ideologies is therefore personal although their basis is social.—L.B. Brown

Ideology arises in association with processes of communication and exchange. Ideology involves the reproduction of the existing relations of production (those activities by which a society guarantees its own survival). Ideology operates as a constraint, limiting us to certain places or positions within these processes of communication and exchange. Ideology is how the existing ensemble of social relations represents itself to individuals; it is the image a society gives of itself in order to perpetuate itself.—Bill Nichols.

According to Marx, it is not necessary to be a shop-keeper or to identify with the class interests of shopkeepers in order to represent the ideology of the petty bourgeoisie: one does not have to be a member of a specific class to share its ideology. There are countless examples in the past of artists who adopted the ideology of their masters and patrons, not out of duty of convention, but conviction and devotion.
—Arnold Hauser

The ideology of the white-collar people rises rather directly out of their occupations and the requirements for them. They are not a well defined group in any other readily apparent sense. This ideology is not overtly political, yet by political default, it is generally "conservative" and by virtue of the aspects of occupation which it stresses, it sets up "social" distinctions between white-collar and labor and makes the most of them.—C. Wright Mills

The magnetic power exerted by patently threadbare ideologies is to be explained, beyond psychology, by the objectively determined decay of logical evidence as such. Things have come to a pass where lying sounds like truth, truth like lying. Each statement, each piece of news, each thought has been pre-formed by the centres of the culture industry.—Theodor Adorno

By ideology we mean, in its broadest sense, a complex of propositions about the natural and social world which would be generally accepted in a given society as describing the actual, indeed necessary, nature of the world and its events.—Victor Burgin

image

im·age \'im-ij\ n [ME, fr. OF, short for imagene, fr. L imagin-, imago; akin to L imitari to imitate] 1 : a reproduction or imitation of the form of a person or thing; esp : an imitation in solid form 2 a : the optical counterpart of an object produced by a lens, mirror, or other optical system b : any likeness of an object produced on a photographic material 3 : exact likeness 4 a : a tangible or visible representation : INCARNATION b archaic : an illusory form : APPARITION 5 a (1) : a mental picture of something not actually present : IMPRESSION (2) : a mental conception held in common by members of a group and symbolic of a basic attitude and orientation b : IDEA, CONCEPT 6 : a vivid or graphic representation or description 7 a : something introduced to represent something else that it strikingly resembles or suggests b : FIGURE OF SPEECH 8 : a person strikingly like another person

The Age demanded an Image.—Ezra Pound

An image is a sight which has been recreated or reproduced. It is an appearance or a set of appearances, which has been detached from the place and time in which it first made its appearance and preserved—for a few moments or a few centuries. Yet, although every image embodies a way of seeing, our perception or appreciation of an image depends also upon our own way of seeing.—John Berger

We live in a swirl of images and echoes that arrest experience and play it back in slow motion.
—Christopher Lasch

Creative exploration in the arts has yielded significant parallels with scientific investigation. The early twentieth-century painters who were still hoping and trying to embrace the complete vista of contemporary conditions looked for structural principles in *art*. Instead of aiming at an illusionary rendering of what they could see around them, they invented *images* and *patterns*.—Gyorgy Kepes

Cameras define reality in the two ways essential to the workings of an advanced industrial society: as a spectacle (for masses) and as an object of surveillance (for rulers). The production of images also furnishes a ruling ideology. Social change is replaced by a change in images.—Susan Sontag

The entire mental panorama in which man is situated is produced by technicians and shapes man to a technological universe, the only one reflected toward him by anything represented to him. Not only does he live spontaneously in the technological environment, but advertising and entertainment offer the image, the reflection, the hypostasis of that environment.
—Jacques Ellul

information

in·for·ma·tion \,in-fər-'mā-shon\ n 1 : the communication or reception of knowledge or intelligence 2 a : knowledge obtained from investigation, study, or instruction b : INTELLIGENCE, NEWS c : FACTS, DATA d : a signal (as one of the digits in dialing a telephone number) purposely impressed upon the input of a communication system or a calculating machine 3 : the act of informing against a person 4 : a formal accusation of a crime made by a prosecuting officer as distinguished from an indictment presented by a grand jury 5 : a numerical quantity that measures the uncertainty in the outcome of an experiment to be performed

Information: Any difference that makes a difference.
—Gregory Bateson

Information is a name for the content of what is exchange with the outer world as we adjust to it, and make our adjustment felt upon it. . . . To live effectively is to live with adequate information.
—Norbert Wiener

. . . the jargon of information technology itself (being relatively new) is so extensive that a special English-German dictionary of 10,000 words was published in 1968 and recently updated to 15,000 items.—Daniel Bell

We are constantly taking information given in one form and translating it into alternative forms, searching for ways to map strange new phenomena into simpler and more familiar ones. The search is something we call 'thinking'; if we are successful, we call it 'understanding'.—George A. Miller

When I'm drivin' in my car
And that man comes on the radio
And he's telling me more and more
About some useless information
Supposed to fire my imagination
     I can't get no
     Satisfaction
—Mick Jagger

media   message

media *pl of* MEDIUM

me·di·um \'mēd-ē-əm\ *n, pl* mediums *or* me·dia \-ē-ə\ [L, fr. neuter of *medius* middle — more at MID] **1 a :** something in a middle position **b :** a middle condition or degree : MEAN **2 :** a means of effecting or conveying something: as **a** (1) **:** a substance regarded as the means of transmission of a force or effect (2) **:** a surrounding or enveloping substance **b** (1) **:** a channel of communication (2) *media pl but sometimes sing in constr* **:** a publication or broadcast that carries advertising **c :** GO-BETWEEN, INTERMEDIARY **d :** an individual held to be a channel of communication between the earthly world and a world of spirits **e :** material or technical means of artistic expression **3 a :** a condition in which something may function or flourish **b** (1) **:** a nutrient system for the artificial cultivation of bacteria or other organisms or cells (2) **:** a fluid or solid in which organic structures are placed **c :** a liquid with which pigment is mixed by a painter **4 :** a size of paper usu. 23 x 18 inches **syn** see MEAN

. . ."the medium is the message" because it is the medium that shapes and controls the scale and form of human association and action. The content or uses of such media are as diverse as they are ineffectual in shaping the form of human association.
—Marshall McLuhan

We must understand communication as something other than the simple transmission—reception of a message, whether or not the latter is considered reversible through feedback. Now, the totality of the existing architecture of the media founds itself on this latter definition: They are what always prevents response, making all processes of exchange impossible. . . .—Jean Baudrillard

True pluralism in our mass media would first of all involve the working and the creative presence in the industries of the real artists and writers of the country. There are serious and possibly embarrassing questions that might be asked of the owners and producers of these media. How interested are they in bringing into their industries the artists and other persons of superior imaginative talent of the country? To what extent have they surrendered the thinking in these media to the idea men of Madison Avenue?—William F. Lynch

The Hutchins Commission set up five main requirements for the mass media in their 1947 report, and, after submitting the American media to these standards, concluded that they were not really socially responsible. The Commission maintained that the media of the United States should:
1. present a "truthful, comprehensive and intelligent account of the day's events in a context which gives them meaning";
2. provide a "forum for the exchange of comment and criticism";
3. project a "representative picture of the constituent groups in the society";
4. present and clarify "the goals and values of the society"; and
5. give "full access to the day's intelligence."
—John C. Merril/Ralph L. Lowenstein

mes·sage \'mes-ij\ *n* [ME, fr. OF, fr. ML *missaticum*, fr. L *missus*, pp. of *mittere*] **1 :** a communication in writing, in speech, or by signals **2 :** a messenger's errand or function

["The medium is the message"] tells us that the bourgeoisie does indeed have all possible means at its disposal to communicate something to us, but that it has nothing more to say. It is ideologically sterile. Its intention to hold on to the control of the means of production at any price, while being incapable of making the socially necessary use of them, is here expressed with complete frankness in the superstructure. It wants the media *as such* and *to no purpose.*
—Hans Magnus Enzenberger

For their part, television stations 'recruit' an audience for advertisers, which is not difficult since they have what amounts to a government-protected monopoly over one of a limited number of channels in the area, or "market." In turn, advertisers, who are the sole paying customers for television stations, buy minutes of time on these programs to convey messages about their products to potential customers.
—Edward Jay Epstein

Mass Communications are now a pillar of the emergent imperial society. Messages "Made in America" radiate across the globe and serve as the ganglia of national power and expansionism. The ideological images of "Have-not" states are increasingly in the custody of American informational media.
—Herbert Schiller

The commitment openly declared, and the message appropriately communicated, are always conscious of their intention and meaning, and they will be consciously accepted or rejected by the recipient.
—Arnold Hauser

propaganda

pro·pa·gan·da \,präp-ə-'gan-də, ,prō-pə-\ n [NL, fr. *Congregatio de propaganda fide* Congregation for propagating the faith, organization established by Pope Gregory XV] **1** *cap* : a congregation of the Roman curia having jurisdiction over missionary territories and related institutions **2** : the spreading of ideas, information, or rumor for the purpose of helping or injuring an institution, a cause, or a person **3** : ideas, facts, or allegations spread deliberately to further one's cause or to damage an opposing cause; *also* : a public action having such an effect

Propaganda must be total. The propagandist must utilize all of the technical means at his disposal—the press, radio, TV, movies, posters, meetings, door-to-door canvassing. Modern propaganda must utilize *all* of these media. There is no propaganda as long as one makes use, in sporadic fashion and at random, of a newspaper article here, a poster or a radio program there, organizes a few meetings and lectures, writes a few slogans on walls; that is not propaganda.
—Jacques Ellul

Questions of psychology are exclusively the concern of the Propaganda Ministry. . . .—Goebbels

Regardless of which of the many definitions one is examining, he finds certain core ideas about propaganda: "manipulation," "purposeful management," "preconceived plan," "creation of desires," "reinforcement of biases," "arousal of preexisting attitudes," "irrational appeal," "specific objective," "arousal to action," "predetermined end," "suggestion," and "creation of dispositions."
—John C. Merril/Ralph L. Lowenstein

In propaganda as in advertising, the important consideration is not whether information accurately describes an objective situation but whether it sounds true.—Christopher Lasch

Art contains propaganda, assertion and intent if the artist expresses his political views in such a way that they remain indistinguishable and separable from the strictly aesthetic factors of his work.—Arnold Hauser

The content of propaganda is not science any more than the object represented in a poster is art. The art of the poster lies in the designer's ability to attract the attention of the crowd by form and color. A poster advertising an art exhibit must direct the attention of the public to the art being exhibited; the better it succeeds in this, the greater is the art of the poster itself. The poster should give the masses an idea of the significance of the exhibition, it should not be a substitute for the art on display. Anyone who wants to concern himself with the art itself must do more than study the poster; and it will not be enough for him just to saunter through the exhibition. We may expect him to examine and immerse himself in the individual works, and thus little by little form a fair opinion. A similar situation prevails with what we today call propaganda.—Adolf Hitler

This astounding volume of propaganda for commodities is often untruthful and misleading; and is addressed more often to the belly or to the groin than to the head or to the heart.—C. Wright Mills

science

sci·ence \'sī-ən(t)s\ n [ME, fr. MF, fr. L *scientia*, fr. *scient-, sciens* having knowledge, fr. prp. of *scire* to know; akin to L *scindere* to cut — more at SHED] **1 a** : possession of knowledge as distinguished from ignorance or misunderstanding **b** : knowledge attained through study or practice **2 a** : a department of systematized knowledge as an object of study (the ~ of theology) **b** : something (as a sport or technique) that may be studied or learned like systematized knowledge **c** : one of the natural sciences **3** : knowledge covering general truths or the operation of general laws esp. as obtained and tested through scientific method; *specif* : NATURAL SCIENCE **4** : a system or method based or purporting to be based upon scientific principles **5** *cap* : CHRISTIAN SCIENCE

"Science" comes to us from those academic Dark Ages when men had to console themselves for their ignorance by pretending that there was a limited amount of knowledge in the world, and little chaps in caps and gowns strutted about, bachelors who knew a passable lot, masters who knew a tremendous lot, and doctors in crimson gowns who knew all that there was to be known. Now it is manifest that none of us knows very much, and the more we look into what we think we know, the more hitherto undetected things we shall find lurking in our assumptions. Hitherto this business of research, which we call the "scientific world," has been in the hands of very few workers indeed.
—H.G. Wells

The figure of 8 million scientific documents yearly put into circulation in 1985 as against 2 million in 1970 must therefore be considered as a conservative forecast. A mere continuation of the present tendency (1967-1971) would produce a total of some 13 to 14 million per year, i.e. equivalent to the stock accumulated since the origins of science until the present day. A projection midway between these figures would seem fairly reasonable.—Daniel Bell

As scientific knowledge increasingly became a crucial determinant of industrial advance and competitive strength, the large industrial firms which had been created to extend and dominate markets, stabilize prices, integrate productive activity, and provide ready returns for speculators and financiers, undertook also to secure control over science.—David Noble

We have accumulated so vast and complex a store of scientific knowledge today that we need a new kind of science to describe the essential motifs of the whole in a unity. Art can make an important contribution by providing insights into structural correspondence common to the various disciplines of science but ignored because science, of necessity, has isolated and limited its fields and objectives.—Gyorgy Kepes

In recent years most working people have acquired a critical sense of the role of science and technology despite a tradition of science mystification and deference to authority. Many now recognize that unemployment, pollution, and disease are another side of the grand hype that science means automatic progress; they see that most of those white-coated experts are owned by business or government. Technology's record has fostered this disillusionment, witness: PCBs, kepone, SST, Tris, nuclear power, occupational hazards, etc.—Scott Thatcher/Bob Park

Control over science ultimately rests in the hands of a powerful ruling elite which functions in its behalf. Science and technology are used as tools for extending the present social and economic system: they have served to increase the wealth and power of the few at the expense of the many. In this context science can never be considered politically neutral.
—*Science for the People*

¹so·ci·ety \sə-'sī-ət-ē\ n [MF societé, fr. L societat-, societas, fr. socius companion — more at SOCIAL] 1 : companionship or association with one's fellows : friendly or intimate intercourse : COMPANY 2 : a voluntary association of individuals for common ends; esp : an organized group working together or periodically meeting because of common interests, beliefs, or profession 3 a : an enduring and cooperating social group whose members have developed organized patterns of relationships through interaction with one another b : a community, nation, or broad grouping of people having common traditions, institutions, and collective activities and interests 4 a : a part of a community that is a unit distinguishable by particular aims or standards of living or conduct : a social circle or a group of social circles having a clearly marked identity ⟨move in polite ~⟩ ⟨literary ~⟩ b : a part of the community that sets itself apart as a leisure class and that regards itself as the arbiter of fashion and manners 5 a (1) : a unit assemblage of plants usu. of a single species or habit within an association (2) : ASSOCIATION 6 b : the progeny of a pair of insects when constituting a social unit (as a hive of bees); broadly : an interdependent system of organisms or biological units

Since society exists as both objective and subjective reality, any adequate theoretical understanding of it must comprehend both these aspects.
—Peter L. Berger and Thomas Luckmann

The history of all hitherto existing society is the history of class struggle.—Karl Marx

No society has a monopoly on observation, reflection, or invention. Transmission of experience from society to society multiplies the opportunity for experimentation, for innovation and development.
—Ray L. Birdwhistell

It is the thesis of this book [*Cybernetics and Society*] that society can only be understood through a study of the messages and the communication facilities which belong to it; and that in the future development of these messages and communication facilities, messages between man and machines, between machines and man, and between machine and machine, are destined to play an ever-increasing part.—Norbert Weiner

What characterizes the so-called advanced societies is that they today consume images and no longer, like those of the past, beliefs; they are therefore more liberal, less fanatical, but also more "false" (less "authentic")—something we translate, in ordinary consciousness, by the avowal of an impression of nauseated boredom, as if the universalized image were producing a world that is without difference (indifferent), from which can rise, here and there, only the cry of anarchisms, marginalisms, and individualisms: let us abolish the images, let us save immediate Desire (desire without mediation).—Roland Barthes

It is frequently said that we live in a consumers' society, and since, as we saw, labor and consumption are but two stages of the same process, imposed upon man by the necessity of life, this is only another way of saying that we live in a society of laborers.
—Hannah Arendt

sys·tem \'sis-təm\ n [LL systemat-, systema, fr. Gk systēmat-, systēma, fr. synistanai to combine, fr. syn- + histanai to cause to stand — more at STAND] 1 : a regularly interacting or interdependent group of items forming a unified whole ⟨number ~⟩: as a (1) : a group of interacting bodies under the influence of related forces ⟨gravitational ~⟩ (2) : an assemblage of substances that is in or tends to equilibrium ⟨thermodynamic ~⟩ b (1) : a group of body organs that together perform one or more vital functions ⟨digestive ~⟩ (2) : the body considered as a functional unit c : a group of related natural objects or forces ⟨river ~⟩ d : a group of devices or artificial objects or an organization forming a network esp. for distributing something or serving a common purpose ⟨telephone ~⟩ ⟨heating ~⟩ ⟨park ~⟩ ⟨highway ~⟩ e : a major division of rocks usu. larger than a series and including all formed during a period or era f : a form of social, economic, or political organization or practice ⟨capitalist ~⟩ 2 : an organized set of doctrines, ideas, or principles usu. intended to explain the arrangement or working of a systematic whole ⟨Newtonian ~ of mechanics⟩ 3 a : an organized or established procedure : METHOD ⟨touch ~ of typing⟩ b : a manner of classifying, symbolizing, or schematizing ⟨taxonomic ~⟩ ⟨decimal ~⟩ ⟨~ of musical notation⟩ 4 : harmonious arrangement or pattern : ORDER ⟨bring ~ out of confusion —Ellen Glasgow⟩

With the binary system, a choice must be made, it is constantly *yes* or *no*.—Jacques Ellul

A significant portion of the products of modern technology, especially in the twentieth century, are of unprecedented complexity. They are composed of hundreds, if not thousands, of parts, and may be viewed as complex technical systems, often hierarchically integrated. Yet, it is not the sheer *number* of parts that produces this unprecedented level of complexity— after all, some of the great Egyptian pyramids have over two million blocks— but that the parts in many modern technics are highly differentiated in nature and function and thus require extraordinary integration, a key determinant of complexity.
—N. Bruce Hannay/Robert McGinn

. . .while studies of meaning received all our attention, another definition of art, as a system of formal relations, thereby suffered neglect. This other definition matters more than meaning. In the same sense speech matters more than writing, because speech precedes writing, and because writing is but a special case of speech.—George Kubler

Unlike all previous communications technologies, radio and television were systems primarily devised for transmission and reception as abstract processes, with little or no definition of preceding content. It is not only that the supply of broadcasting facilities preceded the demand; it is that the means of communication preceded their content.—Raymond Williams

. . .It begins to look like some marginal part of a vast, alien realm called "the economy" which is dominated by machines and machine systems, by complex technicalities that can only be understood by those who draw upon data banks and computer networks. The only human involvement that matters significantly in this mammoth economic mechanism is not the lowly task of "working," but professional specialties like "managing," "planning," "consulting," "programming," "decision making"—highly refined skills whose prestige is predicated upon what mechanized systems cannot do . . . *yet*.—Theodore Roszak

. . .the view of the ancients is clearer in so far as they have a clear and acknowledged terminus, while the modern system tries to make it look as if everything were explained.—Ludwig Wittgenstein

technology

tech·nol·o·gy \-jē\ n [Gk technologia systematic treatment of an art, fr. techno- + -logia -logy] 1 : technical language 2 a : applied science b : a technical method of achieving a practical purpose 3 : the totality of the means employed to provide objects necessary for human sustenance and comfort

Technology is the new tail which wags the dog. We are the dog! The non-stop expansion and development of electronics including automatic control and computers set the conditions for the economic, social and political organization of our society. The Consumer Economy is a Computer Economy. The automatic production of goods is dependent upon the use of computers in all phases of administration, manufacture and distribution. Machines controlled by computers have taken over the production of everything from cars to toothpaste, as well as intermediary business transactions. Workers are superfluous. Clerks are unnecessary.—Joseph Berke

Cain was the first plowman. He abandoned sheepherding for technology.—Marshall McLuhan

. . .but the majority of resources is directed toward the development of more sophisticated weapons and counterinsurgency technology (to protect corporate economic interests abroad) and toward automation, information-handling technology, and technologically-induced obsolescence (to maintain the viability of the economic system at home). The use of this technology results in death and destruction, in the waste of natural and human resources, in the fouling of the environment, and in the increased manipulation of society.—*Science for the People*

According to a survey of charter subscribers, [*Technology Illustrated*] the magazine's audience is "interested in the new, but not the outlandish," including such topics as home computers, technology projections for the future, solar architecture, robotics, and energy conservation technologies. The study also showed that 93% of the subscribers were male and the average age was 37.5, with a median household income of $32,448.—*Advertising Age*

Engineers are becoming aware of their crucial role in changing the human environment. Engineers who have become involved with artists' projects have perceived how the artist's insight can influence his directions and give human scale to his work. The artist in turn desires to create within the technological world in order to satisfy the traditional involvement of the artist with the relevant forces shaping society. The collaboration of artist and engineer emerges as a revolutionary contemporary sociological process.
—Robert Rauschenberg and Billy Kluver

How the technology develops from now on is then not only a matter of some autonomous process directed by remote engineers. It is a matter of social and cultural definition, according to the ends sought. From a range of existing developments and possibilities, variable priorities and variable institutions are now clearly on the agenda. Yet this does not mean that the issue is undetermined; the limits and pressures are real and powerful. Most technical development is in the hands of corporations which express the contemporary interlock of military, political and commercial intentions.—Raymond Williams

Definitions from *Webster's Seventh New Collegiate Dictionary*.
Quotations compiled by Peter D'Agostino, Antonio Muntadas, and Berta Sichel.

What's News
The Media in American Society, **Elie Abel**, ed., Institute of Contemporary Studies, San Francisco, CA., 1981.

Minima Moralia
Reflections from a Damaged Life, **Theodor Adorno**, NLB, London, 1974.

Science and Liberation
edited by **Rita Arditti, Pat Brennan, Steve Cavrak**, South End Press, Boston, MA., 1980.

The Human Condition
Hannah Arendt, Doubleday/Anchor Press, New York, 1959.

Alienation, Praxis and Techne in the Thought of Karl Marx
Kostas Axelos, University of Texas Press, Austin/London, 1976.

Image/Music/Text
Roland Barthes, Hill and Wang, New York, 1977.

Mythologies
Roland Barthes, Hill and Wang, New York, 1977.

Camera Lucida
Reflection on Photography. **Roland Barthes**, Hill and Wang, New York, 1981.

Mind and Nature
Gregory Bateson, Dutton, New York, 1979.

For A Critique of the Political Economy of the Sign
Jean Baudrillard, Telos Press, St. Louis, 1981.

The Winging Passage
Daniel Bell, ABT Books, Cambridge, MA., 1980.

Ways of Seeing
John Berger, Penguin Books, 1977.

Counter Culture
Joseph Berke, ed., Peter Owen Limited, Great Britain, 1969.

Kinesics and Context
Ray L. Birdwhistell, University of Pennsylvania Press, Philadelphia, 1970.

Thinking Photography
Victor Burgin, ed., The Macmillan Press Ltd., London/Basingstoke, 1982.

Marx & Engels on the Means of Communications
A selection of texts, edited by **Yves de la Haye**, International General, New York, 1979.

Propaganda
The Formation of Men's Attitudes. **Jacques Ellul**, Vintage Books, New York, 1965.

The Technological Society
Jacques Ellul, Vintage Books, New York, 1964.

The Technological System
Jacques Ellul, Continuum, New York, 1980.

The Meaning of Modern Business
Richard Ells, Columbia University Press, 1960.

The Consciousness Industry
On Literature, Politics and the Media. **Hans Magnus Enzensberger**, A Continuum Book, The Seabury Press, New York, 1974.

News from Nowhere
Edward Jay Epstein, Vintage, New York, 1973.

The Goebbels Diaries 1942/1943
Joseph Goebbels, Doubleday, New York, 1948.

Persuasion
The Theory and Practice of Manipulative Communications. **George N. Gordon**, Communications Art Books, Hasting House, New York, 1971.

Framing and Being Framed
Hans Haacke, The Press of the Nova Scotia College of Art and Design, Halifax/New York University Press, 1975.

Beyond Culture
Edward T. Hall, Doubleday, New York, 1981.

Hegel: On the Arts
Selection from **G. W. F. Hegel's** Aesthetics or the Philosophy of Fine Art, Frederick Ungar Publishing, New York, 1979.

Mein Kampf
Adolph Hitler, Houghton Mifflin, Boston, 1971.

The Sixties
The Art, Attitudes, Politics and Media of our Most Explosive Decade, **Gerald Howard**, ed., Washington Square Press/Pocket Books, New York, 1982.

Structure In Art and In Science
Gyorgy Kepes, ed., George Braziller, New York, 1965.

Subliminal Seduction
Wilson Bryan Key, Signet Books, New York, 1973.

The Culture of Narcissism
American Life in an Age of Diminishing Expectations. **Christopher Lasch**, Warner Books, 1979.

The Savage Mind
Claude Levi-Strauss, University of Chicago Press, 1966.

"Appeal For Cultural Equity"
Alan Lomax, *Journal of Communication*, Spring 1977.

The Images Industries
William F. Lynch, Sheed and Ward, New York, 1959.

Reason and Revolution
Herbert Marcuse, Beacon Press, Boston, 1960.

The Aesthetic Dimension
Herbert Marcuse, Beacon Press, Boston, 1977.

Culture Is Our Business
Marshall McLuhan, McGraw-Hill, New York/Toronto, 1970.

Understanding Media
The Extensions of Man. **Marshall McLuhan**, McGraw-Hill, New York, 1964.

Media, Message and Men
New Perspectives in Communications. **John C. Merril/Ralph L. Lowenstein**, Longman, New York/London, 1979.

Aspects of History and Class Consciousness
Isvan Meszaros, ed., Routledge & Kegan Paul, London, 1971.

The Psychology of Communication
George A. Miller, Penguin, Baltimore, 1967.

Power, Politics & People
The Collected Essays of **C. Wright Mills**, Oxford University Press, London/New York, 1967.

Art and Technics
Lewis Mumford, Columbia University Press, New York/London, 1952.

Ideology and the Image
Bill Nichols, Indiana University Press, Bloomington, 1981.

More Sky
Otto Piene, MIT Press, Cambridge/London, 1973.

Teaching as a Conserving Activity
Neil Postman, Delta, New York, 1979.

Person/Planet
Theodore Roszak, Anchor Press, 1979.

Mass Communications and the American Empire
Herbert Schiller, Kelly, New York, 1969.

The Geopolitics of Information
How Western Culture Dominates the World. **Anthony Smith**, Oxford University Press, New York, 1980.

Karl Marx on Society and Change
edited and with an introduction by **Neil J. Snelser**, The University of Chicago Press, Chicago/London, 1973.

On Photography
Susan Sontag, Farrar, Straus and Giroux, New York, 1973.

The Human Uses for Human Beings
Cybernetics and Society. **Norbert Weiner**, Avon/Discus, New York, 1967.

Television: Technology and Cultural Form
Raymond Williams, Schocken, New York, 1974.

Decoding Advertising
Judith Williamson, Marion Boyars Publishers, London/Boston, 1978.

Advertising Age
May 1982